KU-175-276

PENGUIN MODERN CLASSICS

In Love

Alfred Hayes was born into a Jewish family in Whitechapel, London in 1911. A few years later, the family moved to New York, where Hayes grew up, went to college and subsequently worked as a reporter and broadcaster. He also began to write verse, including the poem 'I Dreamed I Saw Joe Hill Last Night', which was later set to music and became a hit for Joan Baez. When the war broke out, Hayes joined the US army and left for Europe. Staying on in Rome after the end of the conflict, he became involved in the neo-realist film movement and worked on the scripts of several classics, including Roberto Rossellini's *Paisà* (1946) and Vittorio De Sica's *Bicycle Thieves* (1948). Rome was also the backdrop for his first two published novels, *All Thy Conquests* (1946) and *The Girl on the Via Flaminia* (1949). In the late 1940s, Hayes moved to Hollywood and worked in the movie business as a screenwriter. His scriptwriting credits include the films *Clash by Night*, *The Lusty Men* and *A Hatful of Rain*, as well as *The Twilight Zone* and *Alfred Hitchcock Presents* for television. He was nominated for two Academy Awards, first for *Paisà* and later for *Teresa* (1951). In 1953, his great novel *In Love* appeared and was widely praised by such influential figures as Antonia White, Elizabeth Bowen, Stevie Smith and Julian Maclaren-Ross. In total, Hayes wrote seven novels, including *My Face for the World to See* (1958) and *The End of Me* (1968). He died in 1985.

ALFRED HAYES

In Love

PENGUIN BOOKS

PENGUIN CLASSICS

UK | USA | Canada | Ireland | Australia
India | New Zealand | South Africa

Penguin Books is part of the Penguin Random House group of companies
whose addresses can be found at global.penguinrandomhouse.com

First published 1953
First published in Penguin Classics 2017
001

Copyright © Marietta Hayes, 1987

Set in 11.25/14 pt Dante MT Std
Typeset by Jouve (UK), Milton Keynes
Printed in Great Britain by Clays Ltd, St Ives plc

A CIP catalogue record for this book is available from the British Library

ISBN: 978–0–241–30713–7

www.greenpenguin.co.uk

MIX
Paper from
responsible sources
FSC® C018179

Penguin Random House is committed to a
sustainable future for our business, our readers
and our planet. This book is made from Forest
Stewardship Council® certified paper.

Love bade me welcome, yet my soul drew back,
  Guilty of dust and sin.
But quick-eyed Love, observing me grow slack
  From my first entrance in,
Drew nearer to me, sweetly questioning
  If I lacked anything.

— GEORGE HERBERT

I

Here I am, the man in the hotel bar said to the pretty girl, almost forty, with a small reputation, some money in the bank, a convenient address, a telephone number easily available, this look on my face you think peculiar to me, my hand here on this table real enough, all of me real enough if one doesn't look too closely.

Do I appear to be a man, the man said in the hotel bar at three o'clock in the afternoon to the pretty girl who had no particular place to go, who doesn't know what's wrong with him, or a man who privately thinks his life has come to some sort of an end?

I assume I don't.

I assume that in any mirror, or in the eyes I happen to encounter, say on an afternoon like this, in such a hotel, in such a bar, across a table like this, I appear to be someone who apparently knows where he's going, assured, confident of himself, and aware of what, reasonably, to expect when he arrives, although I could hardly, if now you insisted on pressing me, describe for you that secret destination.

But there is one. There must be one. We must behave, mustn't we, as though there is one, cultivating that air of moving purposely somewhere, carrying with us that faint preoccupation of some appointment to be kept, that appearance of having a terminal, of a place where, even while we are sitting here drinking these daiquiris and the footsteps are all quieted by the thick pleasant rugs and the afternoon dies, you and I are expected, and that there's somebody there, quite important, waiting impatiently for us? But the truth is, isn't it, that all our purposefulness is slightly bogus, we haven't any appointment at all, there isn't a place where we're really expected or hoped for, and that nobody's really waiting, nobody at all, and perhaps there never was, not even in the very beginning, long ago, when we hurried even faster than we do now, and there was in us something that permitted us to believe, even for a short while, when we were younger – or at least I was; you, of course, are still comparatively young; how old are you, actually: twenty-four, twenty-five? – that the intensity with which we set out must compel such a destination to exist.

So now, close to forty, I tell myself that perhaps there isn't, and hasn't ever been, a place at all, thinking that to be, not disillusioned, but just the opposite of illusioned, is a sort of improvement, when it probably isn't; and with this sense, that's hard to describe, of permanent loss; of having somewhere committed an error of a kind or a mistake of a kind that can never be rectified, of having made a gesture of a sort that can never be retracted.

But you're pretty. And it's close to four o'clock. And here are the cocktails on the table. And in that mirror both of us are apparently visible. The waiter will arrive when we want him, the clock tick, the check will be paid, the account settled, the city continue to exist.

And isn't that, after all, what we really want?

Things in their place; a semblance of order; a feeling, true or deceptive, of well-being; an afternoon in which something apparently happens.

Nothing shaken; nothing really momentous; a certain pleasure, without a certain guilt.

The guilt comes later, doesn't it? The guilt's further down the menu. It's only when, after the waiter's been paid and the bill settled, that something's always somehow left over, unaccounted for, and that's when we come to the guilt, don't we?

Odd, though, the man said to the pretty girl, how I sleep well, how unimpaired my appetite is, and yet I seem always tired now; there are inexplicable pains in my back, here, where the muscles seem mysteriously knotted, my eyes (although I hardly ever read now, and hardly ever go to the movies) ache; how a rough, dry taste's settled in my mouth.

And why? the man said, having promised to tell her a story, smiling at her, with an odd sort of restraint, looking at the pretty girl who had all the advantages of being not yet forty, and all the disadvantages, why should I feel this way? What have I lost that cannot, supposedly, be recovered? What have I done, he said, to be so unhappy, and yet not to be convinced that this unhappiness, which invests me like an atmosphere, is quite real or quite justified?

Perhaps, the man said, frowning now, to the pretty girl, that's the definite thing that's wrong with me, if something's wrong; I don't know, any more, what things signify; I have difficulty now identifying them; a sort of woodenness has come over me. There they are, the objects that comprehend my world, and here I am, unable to name them any more – an ornithologist to whom all birds have identical feathers, a gardener whose flowers are all alike. Do you think, the man said, earnestly, that's my malady, if it is a malady? My disease, provided it is a disease?

Yes, the man said, I've often wondered why I impress people as being altogether sad, and yet I insist I am not sad, and that they are quite wrong about me, and yet when I look in the mirror it turns out to be something really true, my face is sad, my face is actually sad, I become convinced (and he smiled at her, because it was four o'clock and the day was ending and she was a very pretty girl, it was astonishing how gradually she had become prettier) that they are right after all, and I am sad, sadder than I know.

He began the story.

2

She inhabited a small apartment. Next door, I recall, there was a rather queer girl, New England-looking and tubercular; downstairs, there were a pair of elegant boys who were in television together, and had black candles over an imitation fireplace, and prints on the wall of the muscular guards at Buckingham Palace; a Mrs O'Toole had a dog.

Tiny and high up, her windows faced toward a large office building, and there were always eyes, distantly lascivious, which lifted hopefully from desks or machines or shipping-room tables whenever her curtains stirred. At night she would lock her windows, as well as curtain them, because she had the idea that a prowler (in her dreams he was always a Negro) might lower himself from the roof (she would be asleep, of course, and alone, and it would all be done noiselessly) to the rather wide window ledge and break into the living room in which she slept. I used to try to reassure her about the prowler by pointing out how nearly impossible the feat was, and how close by people were. Mrs O'Toole's dog could bark; at what? she said, it hasn't a tooth in its head; the girl next door could hear if she screamed; but there's something wrong with the girl, she said: she never goes out of that apartment; well, there were the boys downstairs; my God, she said, who could they scare? So I would argue then that the street she lived on was a populated street, and noisy with trucks and buses, and it was not as though she were alone. She was protected, if people were a protection; she was hemmed about, if being hemmed about were a reassurance; she was guarded, if having neighbors who drank too much, and a subway at the corner, and a hack stand with sleepy-eyed hackies reading the late tabloids in their parked cabs were any sort of a guard.

But she had had the usual terrifying experiences. Once, in a local movie house, when she had used the ladies' room; she had screamed then, in absolute panic, seeing the face lifting itself horribly above the edge of the door. And once, in her own apartment. She had heard footsteps in the hallway, very soft and guarded, the insistent creaking of the stairs, a low sound of human breathing. And then a knock. Her door was bolted (and later, when we quarreled, I remember her face appearing in the cautious slit) and chained. She stood there, I used to imagine her standing there, in the short white soiled terrycloth bathrobe she wore, on the scatter rug, forcing herself to ask in a voice that probably wasn't far from hysteria, Who is it? And then (it was odd how unvariable the phrase was, how graven) the unidentifiable voice answered: It's the man you asked for, and she could hear the doorknob being softly tried. She had, then, retreated swiftly to the telephone which rested on the small coffee table beside the studio couch on which she slept, and telephoned the operator, asking in a voice made quite loud and shaken by her terror for the operator to call the police, loud enough for it to penetrate the door, and the experimenting with the doorknob stopped and she could hear the footsteps, hurried now, going down the flights of stairs. But the image stayed with her of that unidentifiable voice disappearing into a crowd of ordinary-looking people coming up or descending into the subway or pausing for a newspaper at the corner stand or mingling with the heavy faces at the bar in the bar and grill, an unidentifiable voice that would insist, as it tried the doorknob softly again, poised there outside her not completely invulnerable door, It's the man you asked for.

She would often think of moving, or of having bars put on her windows, or of somehow reinforcing her door; but in the end what she did was buy, in a store recommended to her by a doctor, a weapon of a kind which resembled a fountain pen but was actually a tear-gas gun, and this she kept also on the coffee table close to the studio couch, with the telephone and the fruit rotting in a black porcelain bowl and the pack of cigarettes and the cigarette lighter that was a gift from some man. It gave her, I suppose, an idea that she was somewhat protected to know it was there, looking harmless enough, an innocent pen; and she had worked out for herself a small manual of arms should the time come when it would be necessary for her to use it: she would, she thought, having gone over her own military strategy, blind the faceless and nameless and unidentifiable assailant with the gas, while her own mouth and nostrils were covered by a wet cloth, since it had been explained to her that a wet cloth was most effective, and then she would seize the phone and call what, of course, were the equally faceless and nameless and unidentifiable police. She had not yet been forced to use the dangerous weapon; and it lay there with, when one knew what it was, a mildly ominous quality beside the telephone and the bowl of rotting fruit.

The studio couch, with its excess of pillows, was arranged against the wall underneath a Japanese print; beside the radiator, there was a small radio; under the windows, bookshelves; in front of the bookshelves, an armchair; in front of the armchair, a hassock. The bathroom was also small, and always littered: from the curtain rods, her stockings were suspended as limply as hanged men; from the white rod above the sink, her brassiere, with its intricate look, dangled; the towels were not quite clean, and never entirely dry, the Kleenex protruded from its torn box, the toothpaste tube was nearly always uncapped. There were an infinite number of small, and to me, mysterious bottles in the medicine cabinet, jars, vials, peculiar pastes, half empty or almost empty, deodorants and salves, with all the disorder of a pharmacy about to go bankrupt. The kitchen, too, hardly larger than a closet, was littered: the cups unwashed, the icebox with a tendency to get out of order, evidences nearly always of a breakfast eaten too quickly or a dinner put together out of whatever was on the shelf, a bottle of Scotch or a bottle of brandy (somebody's present, of course) in the cupboard. There would be, however, mornings when she would make sporadic and intense efforts to put her place into some sort of order, and once a month a colored girl would arrive to air and mop and ventilate and dust and reassemble; but when I think of her, she seems to exist for me in a debris of hats, jewelry, elaborate shoes, an inscribed book, telephone messages, fruit quietly rotting in a bowl, tasseled pillows, love letters tied with a ribbon and hidden away and taken out and read again and sometimes discarded, candy boxes, and of course portraits: portraits of her child, of herself when she was married, looking altogether like another girl, an ancestor who was remarkably pretty, of her mother on a trip to Florida, of a skating party or a Girl Scout campfire, with the girls in middies and laughing and the campfire in the background, and of a man or two. Everything tossed into the last position or the last hiding place it occupied, as though they'd all been looked at or used or picked up briefly and thought about briefly and the mystery they contained too difficult to unriddle, and thrown back again wherever she happened to be, a drawer or a shelf or the edge of a table; but it seems to me now that all this disorder, so much in evidence, and so little cared about, came from the fact that she considered the life that she was leading then as only temporary. This house, the way she lived, was only a hasty arrangement, thrown together to cover a time in her life which she did not consider too important, and in which she did not feel any necessity for putting things into any sort of final order. The final order had not yet arrived; she was waiting for it to arrive.

She had a tiny scar over the ridge of one eye; an almost imperceptible scar; a bow-and-arrow had done that; and she had not been vaccinated on her arm: that was her mother's desire not to have her marked. Her eyes were, I thought, a lovely blue: dark, and when she was angry, they darkened more. She wore her hair up, high and twisted, with a comb in it, and she never did her eyebrows quite right: they were nearly always penciled, I thought, too long. She claimed she could ride a bicycle. We rode one once, and I went into the back of a truck, but that was at the beginning when it was fun on a Sunday to hire a bicycle. She knew a dozen words in French; she had never learned to drive a car; I measured her once, against a wall, kissing her for each twelve inches, and she was five feet, four and a half inches, without her shoes on, or for that matter her stockings either. She had been born in Oak Park, Illinois, during a snowstorm, and she was the only child in the family, and her father had taught mathematics in a public school. Her father was dead now, and her mother had remarried, a man in the produce business, and the child was with them. Once a month she visited them.

O God, she would say, how mixed up I am, aren't I mixed up? Because she wanted everything, and it seemed to her she had nothing. She wanted what was certainly not too much to ask of even a grudging world: a home, another husband, another child. True, the home, when she allowed herself to think of it, was rather modestly imposing, in the suburbs or near the ocean; and true, the husband, when again she would have one, ought to have money, not necessarily too much of it, but in reassuring amounts, for in her first marriage there had been almost no money at all; and the second child, when its small image took shape for her as she lay on the studio couch in her apartment, which now she did more frequently than ever (there seemed at times almost no reason at all to get up and only the telephone still connected her with hope and possibility and a life that existed somewhere outside), was to be a beautiful, talented, charming, healthy, thoroughly wonderful replica of herself. And, of course, to be happy; that was what she wished most for it; not deliriously happy, she was much too realistic, she told herself, to expect that; but happy, quietly happy, beautifully happy, genuinely happy. Wasn't that little enough to ask? A world notoriously ungenerous could hardly refuse her that. The secret was, of course, to extend toward the invisible benefactor always a diffident palm. Besides, she was beautiful. Men, who said almost everything to her, and if she knew them long enough eventually the truth, always said to her that she was beautiful: it was something she remained for them, always, no matter how many other things she stopped being. Then why was everything so difficult? Why did the diffident palm return empty? Why were the alms she asked, the simple alms, refused her? Why, being beautiful, and why, being young, and why, being reasonably faithful and reasonably good and reasonably passionate, was it so hard to gouge out of the reluctant mountain her own small private ingot of happiness?

Palmists, graphologists, the elderly and slightly bizarre ladies in the cafés who read cards, exercised an irresistible fascination for her. Her eyes widened when they traced in her hand a familiar set of initials; or announced, darkly, her attraction for men with black hair; or found, revealed in her penmanship, a struggle between the impulsive side of her nature and the conventional side. When she was informed by the mystical lady in the sequined dress that her future held a marriage, a disappointment, two children, and that happiness, after a great sorrow, awaited her, as indicated by the cards, her handwriting, or the faint tracings of her lifeline, her small pretty face quickened with pleasure. She enjoyed divination; her character would become for her suddenly dramatic; and she could never be able to resist offering to Madame Clarice, the sympathetic ear, or Princess Silver Star, that faded belle of the inner mysteries, or Karghi, the Egyptian, in a tuxedo and a turban, her eager hand.

Everything that verified for her (even a slightly comic science, for she would say that she didn't really believe those magical readings, although wasn't it startling how Madame Clarice had known she had been divorced?) the importance of her own existence attracted her. There was nothing, really, that interested her more than her own future, and particularly which men would occupy it, what children would fill it, and how much happiness it contained.

And yet, though I smiled, though the eagerness with which she extended her willing palm across a checkered tablecloth amused me, did I have the right to smile? For, after all, this passion for prediction was perfectly natural for her: what she wanted more than anything else was some reassurance that tomorrow would be better for her; that some reward awaited her; that a fulfillment of the dreams she thought she kept so well concealed from others was possible. Suppose Madame Clarice was actually in contact with the unknown? Hadn't she, when one considered it, discovered without any hint the former marriage, and hadn't she seen in her palm the existence of a child? Suppose Karghi, the Egyptian, had a special insight? The universe was unknowable, she was unknowable to herself, doubt and accident surrounded one, nothing was certain; how nice if it were true that Princess Silver Star could read or trace or divine the secret future; how, she thought, fair it would be.

If only she were smarter, she'd say. If only she were wiser.

(Because intelligence, too, was the possession of a magical instrument that made the world easier to control, an Aladdin's lamp or a formula for making gold.) Or she would bewail the fact that she had so few friends: was it because of something in her, some coldness, some lack of good will, or was it simply that friends, true friends, by which she meant someone who did not disapprove of what you did, were so rare? She had grown, she thought, so tired of the actual life she led. Everyone seemed more fortunate than she was, luckier, possessing at least something she lacked. She would explain to me frequently how when she was alone or blue or the curse was coming on there were times when the attachments which held her to life seemed almost to have worn away; when she felt as though she existed nowhere, but hung, by a strange suspension, between the dull glare of heaven and the weightless heaviness of earth. It was almost as if, were she to close her eyes long enough, and lie perfectly still in bed, she would drift away, with a kind of levitation, as though she were all hollow and transparent. Then it seemed as though all the thoughts she had ever had, memories and recollections and ideas of people and things, were gone forever from her mind; and as though the beating of her heart had become completely inaudible; and as though the blood had stopped moving in her veins.

She was all glass then, through which she felt one could see, or a girl made of gauze that a breath, the slightest of winds, could blow away. And I, afraid that moods like these, for it seemed to me they were simply moods, were connected with ideas of death, would urge her to do something, for it seemed to me that it was idleness more than anything else which induced in her this sense of nothingness. But she had never really wanted to die; at least she said she had never really wanted to die; that, oddly enough, the drifting away was not connected in her mind with death at all, but with something else, an idea of a kind of joy, of being, finally, free, and that if she ever were to feel free it would resemble that sensation she had when she was least attached to the world. It was a difficult feeling for her to explain, although she tried to convey to me a sensation I rarely experienced, for it wasn't being free from the world I wanted but being in control of it, and I would urge her then, hardly knowing what to recommend, to fill her days with something she cared about; and then she would try to think, deliberately, what it was she cared about.

She had played the piano when she was small; now she no longer played the piano; she thought how nice it would be, how comforting, during the long afternoons, to have a piano again; but it was much too difficult to go about the intricate (or so it seemed to her) business of renting one, and besides, the apartment was too small. Nevertheless, one of her unhappinesses was the missing piano. She had also been an excellent swimmer when she was a child; or so it seemed to her now, thinking of the summers she had spent at the beach, or the country resorts; and she thought if there were something she could do again, like swimming or mountain climbing, something very active, how much happier she'd be. But the pools far down in the gloomy interiors of the big hotels were so damp, and so small, and so unattractive; and then, the getting out of one's clothes, and the whole dreariness of renting a towel, and having one's hair wet all day, it was too much; nevertheless, one of her unhappinesses was the vanished swimming.

Meanwhile, the traffic below continued as it always had: the trucks, ignoring her lack of joy, rolled their huge wheels up the dirty inclines of the warehouses; the buses, unaware of her melancholy, pulled up at their scheduled stops; the subway expresses came and departed, all without any knowledge of her.

I realize now that I had accustomed myself, without admitting it, to thinking of her as being always in this place, in these surroundings; that to me the studio couch and the drapes drawn to protect her from either the real or the imaginary Peeping Toms, and even the disorder of her medicine cabinet, were permanent. She would exist among these love letters and these portraits for as long as I loved her. I did not, of course, think of myself as loving her forever, but neither did I think of the time when I would stop loving her. No, what I thought, I suppose, really, was that this scene would remain forever unchanged: downstairs, in the vestibule, I would ring her bell, the buzzer would answer and release the door, I would climb the familiar stairs, noting the same odor in the hallway, hearing in winter the same concealed hiss of steam, and she would be always there, available, pretty, young, seated with her legs tucked under her on the studio couch among the colored pillows, the radio or the victrola playing; and we would, in those fixed ceremonials, go out to some restaurant, choose a place where we could dance, because she liked to dance, or bored, choose from the always diminishing number of movies we had not seen one that still remained to be seen, taxiing homeward later, and eventually, evening after evening, in the darkness, with the drapes drawn and the lights extinguished, on the studio couch, uncovered now and the pillows scattered on the floor, make love. It was a very convenient and fixed and unvarying idyll I had in mind, a simple sequence of pleasures that would not seriously change my life or interfere with my work, that would fill the emptiness of my long evenings and ease the pressures of my loneliness, and give me what I suppose I really thought of as the nicest amusement in all the amusement park: the pleasure of love.

3

She always insisted that she could remember every detail of the very first evening we were together; how, for example, there was snow falling, and how the taxi meter, a little yellow glow above it, ticked, and how she felt, excited, in the interior of the heated cab, touching hands, but sad too, sad inside, the way you feel when you like a man, and when you know that with him it will happen, and you've made up your mind even before it happens so that he doesn't really have to ask you, it's something (she explained, explaining how a woman in so representative a circumstance feels) you feel and he feels, a pleasurable tension between you, a silken tightness, waiting to get to a place, his apartment or yours or a friend's room or a hotel or even a deserted country road, so that you sink into a trance of waiting, a deliciousness that's somehow sad, too, and you feel, because of the sadness, both there and not there, inside the cab and holding hands and not inside the cab at all and not holding hands at all.

While the fur on her fur coat was shedding.

She looked out of the window of the cab then at the falling and spinning snowflakes, and the dark store fronts, securely bolted against the night, and she said (it was the only phrase I, too, remembered, there were so many other things I had forgotten but the little truncated phrase I remembered) isn't it

beautiful sometimes, and I asked her what was beautiful sometimes, and she said: The snow, and everything.

So that there must have been, for her, a momentary pang of
something lovely, something that the hush of whiteness and
the somnolent heat of the cab gave her. Perhaps it was the
anticipation, that moment sustained by the drive home, when
one is in a taxi with a stranger who is about to be transfigured
into a lover, and there is an interval, as in music, when the
chord of desire has been struck, and the chord of the fulfillment of desire hasn't; when everything remains suspended and
anticipatory, and the snow falls through the air of a city whose
ugliness is temporarily obscured, and the cab itself seems to
exist inside a magical circle of quiet heat and togetherness and
motion; and, I suppose, for that moment, it is beautiful: the
snow, and everything.

It was a weekend I was staying at a midtown hotel. In
the mornings I would walk down to a cafeteria on Third Avenue, buy the morning papers and have a slow breakfast, with
the ball scores and the theater reviews, and after breakfast
I'd walk slowly back to the hotel and try again to work. I was
having at that time a great deal of difficulty writing. I could not
seem to maintain, for the necessary number of hours, a belief
in the thing I was trying to do, and I would sit there, at that tiny
hotel desk, fretful and tormented, struggling to restore to
myself a confidence I had apparently lost. I was sure that it was
not lost forever, for I had had it once, that quick and absorbing
fever, the buoyancy, that certainty that what I was doing was
right and somehow important, somehow necessary, and I
thought that if I were patient enough, obstinate enough, a
lucky stroke or a happy image would restore it for me. So ideas,
deceptively bright, would appear in the desiccated air, and I
would hopefully follow them only to find the waterhole dry
and the palmtrees dead; plots, seemingly foolproof, would

exist briefly and then dissolve; and now the fear came, secretively, that possibly I had come to the end of what I'd had: that the ax, suspended so long above me, had at last fallen: there was my head, in the failure's usual basket.

It was to this hotel I brought her. Downstairs, I recall, the salesmen, who had their regular suites, were sitting in the lobby, their hats on their knees, smoking cigars. The sound of the elevator penetrated the walls of the hotel room, and there was, in the room, one of those cumbersome hotel radios into which one dropped quarters, and whose dial seemed nailed to those smaller city stations which apparently had inexhaustible record libraries of South American music, so that in the room there must have been the sound, later, of all the professional rumbas and sambas, played with too much verve, to fill the silence our being alone made; and when she came toward me, afterward, half closing the bathroom door behind her (for she always needed to have a light somewhere, in the bathroom or in the kitchen, the light apparently giving her a sort of security) I realized I hadn't until then seen how beautiful she was, as now, naked, with her hair unplaited, her arms crossed so that her slender hands inadequately concealed the little pointed breasts, and shivering a little, and anxious a little, and not too sure of herself and of what I would think of her as a lover, she approached the bed.

I suppose no evening is ever again like the very first evening, the nakedness ever again quite the nakedness it is that first time, the initial gestures, hesitant and doubtful and overintense, ever again what they were, for nothing we want ever turns out quite the way we want it, love or ambition or children, and we go from disappointment to disappointment, from hope to denial, from expectation to surrender, as we grow older, thinking or coming to think that what was wrong was the wanting, so intense it hurt us, and believing or coming to believe that hope was our mistake and expectation our error, and that everything the more we want it the more difficult the having it seems to be, though Howard said no, the man she married said no, he said what people wanted most was money, because money represented everything else, but that people were ashamed of having so exclusive a feeling for money, and they concealed this feeling, and in the end possibly even I agreed with him.

She recalled, too (we were sitting on the terrace of the cafeteria in the zoo in Central Park, and a lion was roaring) that when she was at school and was initiated into her sorority, she was blindfolded and somebody tied a string to an oyster and they told her she had to swallow the oyster and she could taste it in her mouth, the awful cold slimy dead taste and she gulped and gulped and when it finally lodged in her throat and she was about to swallow it they tugged the oyster back out and God the sensation was just awful and every time she even saw a plate of oysters sitting on a bed of ice she got ill remembering. And at fourteen (we were eating in a small Italian restaurant off Sixth Avenue and I had spilled some red wine) she had acne and she was fat and she thought she was never going to be slender like the ballet dancers whose photographs clipped from a magazine she had tacked to the wall of her bedroom and then at sixteen she was suddenly slender and very pretty and the acne was all gone and then she realized that her breasts would always be small, that she would never have any sort of an impressive bosom at all and the boys downtown standing outside the drugstore or the candystore would never whistle at her when she walked by and probably nobody would ever be mad about her, really mad, and shoot himself out of sheer love, and she sighed and reconciled herself to it and when she got older nobody ever really did, it would be sort of nice, she thought, to be really madly loved and have somebody actually threaten to kill himself about her, but she supposed it would never happen. And then at seventeen she was married. Incredibly married.

It was the first year (I'd brought flowers and a box of candy, and she was eating the candy, slowly, meditatively) she was really pretty, and New York seemed to her, coming from the small suburban town where her parents were now and where they had the child, the most wonderful city in the world. Nothing was ugly to her then, and all day long she shivered with excitement, the most wonderful things seemed about to happen, and then there was the boy, for she always thought of him as a boy, a boy she had married. And she used to sit, listening to him talk about his childhood, he had a family in Philadelphia, his mother drank, and he used to send her money every month, and she would pity him, her heart aching, there were so many burdens on him, her eyes shining with love and ignorance. She had been (she thought of it now with a little amused touch of bitterness and self-mockery) so willing to do anything, anything he'd ask her to do, take a boat to Africa, live at the Pole, outrage her family, scandalize the world, anything, all in the ache of love and self-sacrifice. (Would she ever feel like that again? She thought not; how could she possibly? The girl who had felt all that was dead. She was quite sure the girl who had glowed like that and been so radiant and such a fool was dead.) So they were married, the following spring, he was only twenty, and they went to Philadelphia to see his mother, and it seemed to her it was what she had always waited so impatiently for: to be married and to have a child. She was only eighteen then, the ward (because they had no money at all, but she thought, being eighteen, that money wasn't the important thing) crowded with women, feeling herself in the neat tucked-in hospital bed immeasurably small, the doctor smiling at her for she

seemed hardly old enough to be lying there, a toy giving
birth to another toy, and then there was the war, the long
journey, carrying the infant and the formula bottles and the
packet of diapers in the dirty overcrowded wartime train
where she had to ask the porter please would it be all right
if she warmed the bottles in the Pullman kitchen, and sway-
ing through the train full of sleeping soldiers and rumpled
civilians to the kitchen and back again to her seat where she
had the child carefully propped in a basket, the journey to
the airbase where he was stationed, and his odd feeling, when
she saw him, about the baby, how now the baby too was a
burden, another burden, like his mother in Philadelphia to
whom inexorably every month part of even his army money
was still sent.

She felt she had tried: it was so difficult, even now, three
years afterward, when she no longer hated or blamed or
accused him, to say why it had happened. Whether one had
been too much in love, or not enough. Whether it was his
childhood – that slum, and the boy helping a drunken mother
into bed; or her inexperience – that shock when the wedding
night was neither wonderful nor transfiguring, but only painful, and the world the next morning showed its old disfigured
face; or their mutual inarticulateness – if she had been able to
speak out, to reach and touch him, or if he had been able to
reach and touch her. She was not sure, even now, why they had
failed, and the marriage had failed. There was only, for her, the
incredible fact, who had never believed anything of the sort
would happen, that it had happened: and here she was, not yet
twenty-two, a mother, divorced, alone.

And she would look at me: did I think what was wrong
was marriage itself? Of course, she had married too young;
she could see that, now. And there had been so much ignorance on both their parts; so much clumsiness; so much

misunderstanding; she thought (sighing) that, after all, what was wiser was not to marry for love, that one always made a better wife when one was not in love, it was love that made marriage so difficult, the sense of failure was so acute then. As for me, she was quite sure that women had always been a little too good to me.

Too good?

Because they'd loved me.

But I'd been in love, too, or thought I had. And I'd spent, as most men had, that is men who cared about women, an unconscionable number of hours, out of the time I had available, loving them, indulging them, or persuading them to go to bed. And besides, love: there were so many other emotions which weren't love at all, but which masqueraded as love, or assumed its name; didn't she agree? And happiness: the suburban hideaway and the bedroom with the chintz curtains; wasn't it possible to aspire to something else, wasn't it conceivable that happiness might not be the single goal?

But what was it, then, I wanted? she would ask, almost angrily, not really believing me (as, possibly, I did not believe myself), thinking that the obstinacy with which I spoke of some vague freedom, without shape, without substance, was only another of my infinite poses; and that it was all bound up (she could not say exactly how or why) with my reluctance to proclaim I loved her (desperately, of course) and could not live without her (when, after all, there were so many girls I had loved and managed to live without). And something would move then in the depths of her eyes; some old resentment stirred. How could one possibly not want happiness? And what could I want from her, then, if what I wanted was not happiness? What else could she, who felt secretly that she had little enough to give, give me if not that which any man, coming to her, alternating the clumsiness of his rhetoric with the mute fumblings at her breast or hip, thought of as happiness? To ask nothing of her (as I was apparently doing) or to demand, or to pretend to demand, nothing, to act out while I kissed her some half-expressed comedy of independence, drew her to me and at the same time stirred in her some inarticulate antagonism, and made her feel, obscurely, some unvoiced denial of herself. So she would say to me, to test my sincerity: Wouldn't it matter to you if I left you? (The smile would be fixed on my face; I would become, when she asked me, conscious of how fixed my smile was.) If I said to you, she would say, watching me carefully, searching my face, now that it was all over between us and I wanted never to see you again, would it make a difference to you? Suppose I said it now, she would say. I would glance at my wrist watch.

At ten-thirty?

And she would answer, yes, at ten-thirty, now, this minute, would I, if she insisted that it was all over between us, irrevocably over, just pick up my hat and go? But I, smiling, was quite sure she wouldn't say it.

Nevertheless, suppose she did? Would it matter, would it matter at all? Yes, it would matter, I said, carefully, very much. How much would it matter? she said. I'd be miserable, I said, knowing that much was true, I'd miss her, very much, and I'd be unhappy, quite unhappy, she could be sure of that; but it was not the assurance that parting from her would upset me, or make me unhappy, which was compelling her, because then she would say that, though I might be miserable for a while, even genuinely unhappy, I'd survive.

Didn't she want me to survive?

And I suppose she didn't; only an absolute sort of incapacitation, if she left me, would have pleased her; nothing, I suppose (for at that time I did not think her going would have really occasioned in me more than a particularly sharp regret), but an extreme of suffering, or even possibly a gentle attempt to hang myself from some convenient chandelier, would have satisfied her that I was truly in love.

Was I?

Was she?

It was true that I was often bored; that she was frequently depressed; that there were nights I sat in the chair opposite her, listening to the radio, or her records, with absolutely nothing to say to her; and there were times when I was restless, when I regretted having begun an affair at all, times I longed to be someplace else than in this small apartment, engaged in those endless and not very interesting duologues that precede going to bed or are interspersed between the silent numbing kisses and the intervals when, exhausted, the bodies of the lovers separate and roll away, each to a side of a disordered bed, and in the dark air, of which one is again conscious, the sexual sweats slowly dry, and the heart, set off like a burglar alarm, finally subsides. Sometimes, hating the violent dispossession of myself which love brought on, I would wish to be elsewhere; and feeling me withdrawn from her, she would ask (as I would ask when I felt her withdrawn) what I was thinking of, and I would reply that I was not thinking of anything; but those fleeting resolutions I would make, as I lay in the darkness, to live differently, or those desires I'd experience for another sort of life, were absurd and untrue, for no sooner would I leave her and find myself ideally alone than I would begin longing for her again. Because I, too, was difficult, easily depressed, changeable, evasive, and perhaps not entirely honest. There was no weakness I did not obstinately maintain I possessed, and I was fond of talking at great length about all the defects of my character, and sometimes, not entirely joking, I would advise her to leave me, but she always suspected this concern on my part for her happiness. She was not sure, after all, that I might not feel a more profound relief at her departing than any grief I might claim. She could not really go until she could feel that her loss would be important. Perhaps if she had been completely convinced that I would be properly broken-hearted she might have been able to end the affair with less than the difficulty it ultimately cost us. The portrait I drew of myself was always unflattering (but was it really unflattering? Wasn't it, actually, by insisting so on my inaccessibility making myself more attractive?); but always, of course, with just a touch of sadness to everything I said, a tincture of disenchantment, a slight dusting over my words of an attractive melancholy, as though I had suffered, long ago, some wound, some profound disappointment. Ah, the roles I played, sitting there in the green armchair of that dwarfed living room, that tiny birdcage with the fruit rotting on the inexpensive coffee table! For now I was the oracle on sex: experienced, objective, clinical. One had always (this with my serious face) certain difficulties due to such and such; there was a girl in Chicago (height, weight, general characteristics) I'd known during a tour; she had had exactly the same experience, in her case an uncle who owned a laundry; and, of course, I had cured her. Naturally. One always implied that there was nothing like a series of treatments, administered by the doctor at this fortunate moment so near one, this most tender of healers, with the miraculous touch, to cure one of a slight inability to enjoy what was really (of course it was!) the simplest, the most available, the nicest of human pleasures. Or again, I was the charming boy, the rosebud who had grown up in a tough neighborhood; or now, the misunderstood or the too much understood; and now, putting my head into her lap, I'd be grateful for the warmth of her flesh, for I was the tired man then, the exhausted hunter home, now love, like a warm laprobe, covered me, and my weary mind relaxed in this simplest of baths. Alternately, I was moody – what was I doing here? Or gay – let's do the town! Or loved her – ah, baby, there's nobody like you! Or mercurial again, did not love her – ah, honeybun, why kid ourselves? Or, retreating, like Hamlet, the distance of her arm, found her an enigma – who are you, after all? A stranger . . . we are all strangers, live, die, breed, stranger with stranger, the unknown copulating with the unknown, mysterious Mr X, the local man in the iron mask, kissing on her palpable mouth the enigmatic Miss X, the beauty nobody knows!

And was this, we say, later, when it's over, really us? But it's impossible! How could that fool, that impossible actor, ever have been us? How could we have been that posturing clown? Who put that false laughter into our mouths? Who drew those insincere tears from our eyes? Who taught us all that artifice of suffering? We have been hiding all the time; the events, that once were so real, happened to other people, who resemble us, imitators using our name, registering in hotels we stayed at, declaiming verses we kept in private scrapbooks; but not us, surely not us, we wince thinking that it could ever have possibly been us.

And I suppose that she, too, in some obscure and difficult way, experienced, in spite of everything, the feeling of her own unreality. She, too, knew the words that came easily or fumblingly were never the true words; everything may have been for her, too, somehow suspect. And yet, by all the orthodoxy of kisses and desire, we were apparently in love; by all the signs, the jealousy, the possessiveness, the quick flush of passion, the need for each other, we were apparently in love. We looked as much like lovers as lovers can look; and if I insist now that somehow, somewhere, a lie of a kind existed, a pretense of a kind, that somewhere within us our most violent protestations echoed a bit ironically, and that, full fathom five, another motive lay for all we did and all we said, it may be only that like a woman after childbirth we can never restore for ourselves the reality of pain, it is impossible to believe that it was we who screamed so in the ward or clawed so at the bedsheets or such sweats were ever on our foreheads, and that too much feeling, finally, makes us experience a sensation of unreality as acute as never having felt at all.

4

One night she had a funny thing happen. Summer had come quickly, the way it always seems to now in New York. The mercury had boiled all day in the public thermometers, and there was an intolerable glitter from the chromework of parked cars. At the traffic intersections, waiting for the signal to change to what seemed a murderously delayed green, you could almost hear the stretched human nerve snap. The city had become, once more, impossible. There were only two habitable places in town that night: an air-conditioned restaurant or a movie, and we had gone into a Lexington Avenue Childs. I'd ordered iced coffee.

The evening before, an evening I had not seen her, she had been out to the Club Paris with a couple she knew, the Whites, Charlie and Isabel, and although she did not like nightclubs, she had always wanted to go to the Club Paris. She had watched the floor-show with an astonished, even slightly awed expression, for it was unbelievable that girls like the girls at the Club Paris, in their feathers, their rhinestones, their pinkness and whiteness, really existed, or that anywhere in the world there were bosoms quite like those which, in quantity, the chorus displayed; it gave her, she said, describing their perfection, the feeling of being almost deformed. Besides, she had gone dressed in a skirt and sweater, because she hadn't expected it to be any sort of an evening, just dinner and a drink, but the

Whites knew so many people, and the people just drifted over. First there was somebody else at the table named Jack who had a girl with him, a rather mannered girl he was supposed to be engaged to, and Charlie White kept making fun of her. It had started out as that sort of an evening, with champagne cocktails, which she loved, and Charlie White saying to Jack's girl, when she talked of some movie actress, Are you an actress? and the girl saying no, she wasn't, she was just sort of interested; and then she'd mention something about the piano player's technique and Charlie White said: Do you play the piano? and it turned out she didn't; and the girl said she liked snow, she was absolutely crazy about snow, and Charlie White asked her: Do you ski? and it turned out she didn't do that either, or paint, or model, or anything: the only thing she apparently did do was have Jack keep her; and then Jack, as he got drunk during the evening, kept saying, She wants me to pay for having her teeth capped but I keep telling her I'll cap them if she'll let me cap the rest of her. Then Charlie White told a story about a guy who unscrewed his navel and his behind fell off and Jack's girl laughed so hard Jack had to pound her back to stop her coughing.

It was that sort of evening, quite brilliant, the kind you groaned at the next day wondering how you could have possibly been that stupid, and then she noticed there was somebody else eating a fillet quietly at the table while the laughter and the jokes continued, who apparently only smiled when he was required to, a rather heavy solid sort of man whom Isabel called Howard, and now and then while he ate, with a steady undisturbed champing of his jaws, he would look at her. Isabel was saying something in reply to something Charlie had said, about men not being any different than women, they all cheated and connived, didn't they? and Charlie answered: Well, they don't suck them dry the way a woman does, when, apparently having finished his fillet and ready now to digest it with a bit of activity, the man Isabel called Howard leaned across the table and asked her to dance. He danced well, but rather heavily; dancing was not, she felt, as he fitted her into his arms, something he particularly enjoyed, but had, obviously – when it became apparent to him that a good part of his life was going to be spent in places where women expected to dance – set himself to reduce as much as possible his natural lack of feeling for it. There were evidently an expensive number of hours at a studio catering to businessmen behind it, but he danced, she thought, rather like a handball, a prescribed sort of movement. For a while, he was silent, concentrated on the music, and she felt, in his arms, quite small, light and fragile. She felt, too, vaguely trapped, the arm about her being somehow too firm and too possessive. The air was layered with cigarette smoke and shot with the colors of a roving spotlight. She hardly knew what to use to begin a conversation; she began to wish the number would be short; and then quite unexpectedly, as though having digested the fillet, and having settled the rhythm of the dance, he had come to what on the agenda was indicated as conversation time, he began to speak to her. Did she go very often to nightclubs? No, she didn't, she replied, but he apparently didn't believe her; a pretty girl like her, and she wasn't invited out frequently? He supposed that all pretty girls were invited out frequently for, after all, that really was why clubs like the Club Paris were built, and why the lights, faint rose or soft yellow, played across the dance floor; didn't she think the lights were romantic? Yes, she did, quite romantic, and then he asked her not to be offended. She wondered briefly what in the world he possibly intended to say that could offend her. But what he said was that she was beautiful, quite beautiful, and obviously meant it; and he pointed out, not intending I suppose any genuine irony, but rather enunciating one of his fixed maxims, that one should be born either beautiful or rich, everything else was a handicap, so that she was left with the feeling that ugliness, poverty, lack of talent, were misfortunes almost all the world, except herself and he, had suffered, and that they were, by these gifts, his money and her beauty, divided from all the unlucky millions. She looked up at that, a little sharply. It was very nice of him to think of her as beautiful, and very flattering, but she did not feel as fortunate as all that. The girls, the magnificent girls in the chorus, the girls in the feathers and rhinestones, who looked so much like creatures one dressed in uncut diamonds; if she looked like the girls in the chorus perhaps what he said might be true, and everything then, perhaps, would be easier than it was.

Was everything difficult now?

She did not know. She guessed not. Difficult? Well, no. Things were, she thought, vaguer than they were difficult. It was just that, looking at the girls, whose navels were perfectly placed, each with its little winking jewel, well one thought that if, by some miracle, one looked like that it must follow that everything must naturally (like a cornucopia pouring out men, automobiles, fur coats, trips to Europe in the spring) come to you.

And he was insisting now, politely: she was beautiful. In a way (though he did not explain how, and allowed her to think she understood without it being explained) he found her kind of beauty preferable; more appealing; she mustn't think that what she had, he said, was less desirable than what the other, more public girls possessed. It was then that she heard him offer her a thousand dollars. And he was quite serious, quite simple about it, it must have seemed to him the most normal of transactions. He was still astonishingly earnest, astonishingly sincere, or apparently sincere, so that the offer, voiced with no more change in him than if he had invited her to dinner, confused her, and he was being, incredibly, she could see, what he thought was genuinely honest and direct, and the money he was offering was, to her, so immense, so unthinkable, that its very size prevented her from being shocked or even offended. She was simply astonished.

Well! she said.

Is that enough? he asked, almost anxiously. He was certainly not trying to cheat her, his concerned face bending toward her as, still dancing, they moved among the couples in each other's arms, intent upon fixing the price fairly, upon not cheating her, and even attempting to convey to her that he wished the dimensions of the money itself to indicate how desirable he thought she was, how genuine his feeling for her was, how honorable he was being.

Enough? she said, incredulously. Oh, dear. And wanted to return now to what seemed the perfect security of the table. But he held her arm a moment longer. Let me give you my card, he said extracting, absurdly, a neatly engraved oblong, and you think about it, pressing it upon her. She experienced now an irresistible desire to giggle. A thousand dollars! For her. Whom nobody ever thought of dressing in uncut diamonds. And his hand, as she tried to disengage herself, on her arm, so that she thought how large it is, imagining it, by some unexpected association, both on the steering wheel of a large powerful hooded car and on her thigh. I won't try to contact you, he said now, softly, as she moved away, through the swirling couples, still being absurd, with that heavy disconcerting thing he thought of as honesty; you decide, he said, my office number's on the card, expecting her to glance at it which she found herself almost doing as, smiling brightly, they approached the table and Isabel, looking up, the pearls about her throat not really masking the faint creases (which she, too, in time, beautiful or not, for Isabel had been as pretty once, still was, would acquire but probably without the masking pearls), said: You looked wonderful together, didn't they, Charlie? and bald, stout, smiling too, with the mustache like a grenadier's, Charlie agreed.

A smile, which identified itself as mine, drifted in the refrigerated air between us; I shook the cubes floating, like miniature bergs, in the tall coffee glass.

You're not intending, I said, to use the card?

Idiot, she said. Of course not. How could I? I was just so overwhelmed by the idea of all that money.

I imagined I would have been, too.

Would you? she said. It is enormous, isn't it? If you were a girl, what would you have done?

Accepted it.

No, she said, seriously. What would you have done?

I didn't know.

A thousand dollars! Oh, God. Barbara (aged five) would have all that money in the bank. She wouldn't touch it. That she wouldn't touch it would purify the money, and she'd put it away, securely, in a safe deposit box somewhere, lock it up, the most secretive of nest eggs, and Barbara would have it when she was seventeen. And that would be nice, wouldn't it, to be Barbara, to be seventeen, and to have, as she had never had, that fine secure feeling of a thousand dollars all her own sitting there waiting in an indestructible bank?

Exceedingly nice, I thought.

Perhaps, she said, as I watched the small blocks of ice diminish in my coffee and invisibly somewhere the machinery that cooled the intense air whirred, I could do it if I were hypnotized, or took some sort of a pill. Was there some sort of a pill or something she could take?

There probably was. I would ask a pharmacist for her; would she like it candy-coated? They made almost all the disagreeable pills nowadays candy-coated, and I was sure that, with a little exertion, I could probably find a pill for her sweet enough to make it all easy. She laughed; and then asked, wide-eyed, if I were jealous; how silly of me to be jealous. How could I, knowing her as I did, and being so perspicacious, imagine that she ever possibly could. Besides, wasn't it I who had insisted that she had a perfect right to go out to dinner with other men, and hadn't it been I who advised her to be independent of me, and assured both of us we were free to do as we chose?

It most certainly had.

He was, she said then, speaking again of Howard, a president of some company. Textiles, she thought, or chemicals, something like that. She wasn't quite sure. But Isabel said he was very rich. Isabel always knew things like that. The first thing Isabel always managed to find out were things like that, how rich they were and pretty exactly too, and I thought Isabel was probably right because he'd have to be, and checking carefully over my memories of even the most munificent night I'd ever spent, in my limited way, of course, and with my modest means, a thousand dollars did seem quite more than even the most luxurious haystack was worth.

Oh, she said, you. How would you know what a woman was worth?

And still I wore that smile that somehow would not fit my face, a smile distributed now among the chicken salads and the stewed vegetables. We both understood that the money, however tempting, was unthinkable, and that what she was being light and gay about, here, in the restaurant, was simply the fact that what had happened was an unusual experience, to be somewhat amazed at, obscurely flattered by, and a little amused with. She looked up now, brightly.

But just think, she said. It would all be over in a night. It was only a night he wanted. I could just forget it and pretend it never happened, couldn't I? And you wouldn't really mind, would you, darling? Because I'd still love you. It wouldn't affect the way I felt about you at all.

She picked at the salad she had ordered.

Reflectively now:

He'd want though, probably, to stick pins in me or something. Don't you think? There must be, it's impossible otherwise, not for a thousand dollars, something funny about him. Pins, that would be horrible.

She sighed.

The small teeth tore at the infinitesimal strips of pallid chicken.

Funny though, she said, how I don't feel outraged. Or disgusted. How I accept it. How it seems perfectly normal for a man I never met before nor even saw, on a dance floor, a Sunday night, to offer me that much money out of the blue. I must be really awful. Suppose my mother knew? She'd die. Tainted money. It would be tainted, wouldn't it?

Yes.

Tainted. What a funny word, she said. And looked at me now, tenderly.

But you'd take me back, wouldn't you, darling? You'd forgive me. After all, I've been nice, haven't I, and I haven't caused you too much trouble, and it's really such a lot of money. Tainted. It is a funny word, isn't it? It sounds like a word my grandmother used to use. What does tainted really mean? Is it like fruit, rotten a bit? But not completely spoiled? Tainted, she said. I'd take the money and I'd be tainted.

She reached across the table, and squeezed my hand. Silly, she said. Stop looking like that. You know I wouldn't.

And it seemed then, with the affectionate gesture, the reassuring smile that accompanied it, the pleasant walk home, that the episode was closed, the incident over; but what incident, where flattery, even of a dubious nature, is involved, is ever over for a woman? What episode, in which she's admired, however obliquely, is ever really ended? She will reopen what seems to you a finished chapter, and manage, somehow, to add a disconcerting epilogue to some drama you assumed was done with quite some time ago.

The heat continued. The city, an enormous pot, cooked its inhabitants over a slow fire. She had gone, as everyone had, through the stunned hours, waiting for the night to obliterate the sun; but the nights were as difficult to endure as the days. She ate little, because of the heat, and slept naked in the tiny living room, and then she had, again, one of her bad dreams.

In the dream she was crossing a street in the small town in which she had been born and to which she returned occasionally, when she noticed a box lying in the gutter. It was a sort of small packing box, and in the dream she realized that her child was in the packing box. It wasn't quite clear to her how the little girl had gotten into the box, although it seemed to her quite logical in the dream that the child should be in the box; she thought, with that odd reasoning with which one accepts the contradictions of a dream, that the child had been playing a game of some kind and had crawled into the small crate to hide; and as she watched, a huge truck came down the street. She found herself powerless as the truck, with a terrible casualness, went over and crushed the crate; and then, when the truck had gone on without stopping or caring, she had rushed into the gutter and had, as she said, the action having some obscure meaning, slid the lid of the crate back, although a crate would not have had a sliding lid. She lifted the little body up, saying Barbara, O Barbara, you're not hurt, although she knew the child was dead; and then she found herself somehow carrying the body in her arms down an endless flight of stairs. She could tell by the way the child lay in her arms that her neck was broken; she was not injured visibly except for the fatal way her neck was, and that was strange too; and as she carried the child she kept saying, O baby, you shouldn't play in the streets, it's so dangerous, you might have been hurt, to reassure the dead little girl because, she felt, if she pretended to the child that she wasn't injured she would not be dead, although she knew the child was. Meanwhile, the endless stairs; and, as she said, the awful atmosphere that surrounded her in the dream which was more terrible, she felt, than the things which the dream actually made happen; and then she woke up. She woke up crying, alone in the room, with the curtains drawn. It was another hot morning. And on the coffee table, where she had forgotten it, close to the fountain pen that contained the capsule of tear gas, lay the engraved card he had given her that night at the Club Paris. She did not think there was any connection between the dream and the decision she made; what she did say was that the dream had exhausted her so much that when she woke up and saw the card lying on the coffee table it seemed so much less terrible than all the other terrible things in the world that could happen to her.

I thought he wouldn't remember me at all when I called, she said. It was four days ago, and I couldn't seem to hold my voice together, but when I called him he seemed to recognize my voice immediately, as though he'd been waiting, as though he'd known I'd wake up and find the card and pick up the phone and call, as though there was nothing else I could do but wake up some morning and call him. He had only to wait, there, in that office of his, sitting in a leather upholstered chair, and I'd do it, just as sure as the sun, not even I suppose really feeling like he'd won anything because he isn't the kind of man who behaves as though there's such a thing as winning or losing, what he thinks is that the world and everybody in it are a certain way, a way he says they are, and when I called I guess I was only doing what he had expected me to do so that there was no question of his being triumphant, he'd just been proven right once again, that was all. And then he said: no, he hadn't been drunk, and yes, of course he remembered what he'd said, and yes, he'd meant it, all as though he thought I was a little hysterical or was going to be hysterical and wanted to calm me down, and I kept saying I wanted to talk about his proposition. Funny, it was the only word I could think of, proposition, I'd never used it before or even dared think of it, but what else could I possibly call it, and that's what it was, wasn't it, a proposition? He didn't seem to like my calling it a proposition, and then he said that it was difficult discussing a matter like we were discussing over the phone, couldn't we possibly go somewhere for a drink? So I met him at the Crystal Room. I suppose there are people in this town that if you have to meet them never can think of any other possible place than 21 or the Stork Club. Do they always meet in places like that, 21 or the Stork Club or the Crystal Room, for everything they do? Business, and everything? I suppose they can't even think of another place. I suppose it just never occurs to them that people do meet other places. I suppose if you insisted they'd think real hard, trying to imagine what place they could slum in, and then they'd say, well, if you like, we can make it at the Waldorf. Anyway, when he arrived, I was already there, and he came over to the table quickly now, smiling and polite, as though it were really an appointment. He had the same sort of blank pleasant earnestness that he had had that night at the Club Paris which upset me so much; I mean, he should have looked different to do what he was doing, or at least sounded different. I suppose I wouldn't have felt comfortable until he twirled his mustaches, waxed ones too, and then I'd have known where I was. Meanwhile, he was ordering a drink; then there was the business of lighting a cigarette, all perfectly normal, but my voice wouldn't change. It was so loud every time I opened my mouth, and I kept wanting him to talk about it. Facts and figures, cold, time, place, arrangements, draw the contract up fast so I could sign it, but he said, still smiling, turning me aside, it could wait, there was no hurry, we had all day.

Not to look at him, she said. That's what I thought. He isn't anything. He's a suit of clothes. He's something in a chair. Because I'd made up my mind to go through with it. He asked me questions. About my family, where were they, what my father did, was I married, was I in love with somebody. I told him it was none of his business. And he just smiled, a suit of clothes with a smile. I hated him for offering me the money. Now I first really hated him. I hadn't hated him that night at the Club Paris because then it was just funny. Unbelievable, that's all. But now I hated him. Because he had no right to make me think all that money was there and I could have it for something as stupid and as unimportant as going to bed with him. He'd made me think: Why shouldn't I? He'd made me say: What difference does it make?

It would be at his apartment, she said. Dinner. I supposed the maid would cook. And candles. Then in the morning I'd leave. I'd have the money in advance. Simple, wasn't it? How nice and simple. And the simpler it seemed, the more I hated him.

And why not, she said. I couldn't think of why not. I go to bed with you, don't I? For love. And you wouldn't really care as long as you didn't know. Who really cares about me? Who gives a damn what I do? Nobody came to me and said: We'll take care of Barbara, don't do it. No. They'd all be shocked. And they'd all envy the money. They'd all think to themselves: What would I have done? If only he'd take me, now, to wherever it was he lived. Quick. Instead, he asked me to dance.

Dance, she said. God, it was the last thing I wanted to do. I'd made him order me another drink. I kept thinking: I'll buy Mother a present with some of it. She hadn't had a present. And the rest I'll put away for Barbara.

So we danced, she said. In the Crystal Room. Tea music, I suppose. He asked me if the ring I was wearing was gold. It was my wedding ring. I said Mother had given it to me. He asked me if I always wore clothes like that. Not that he didn't like the way I dressed; just that it was different. Did I always wear off-the-shoulder things? I said I thought it gave me more height. I said I supposed he had all kinds of money. He said no, only the kind they printed in Washington. He asked me if I had many women friends. I said no. He asked me why. I said I preferred men. He said that he thought women were difficult to understand. I said a woman is what she is. That she has a right to love and a right to be happy and a right to be supported. He said: Why? I said because she bears the children. He looked at me. That doesn't leave a man very many rights, does it? he said. I said he wouldn't talk that way if he had ever been married, and he said he had had that pleasure. He got a funny look on his face. I wondered if his wife was beautiful. He said perhaps, but that all he could remember was that she was a woman. And that condemns her? I said. He didn't answer. Obviously he hadn't been married very long. Oh, he said, yes he had, a long time: almost two days. One day in New York and one day at the Hotel George Cinq in Paris. When they were in the Hotel George Cinq in Paris his wife sat up in bed, drunk on the bridal champagne, and she started to laugh. He had been reasonably sure she was a virgin, or if not precisely a virgin, a facsimile thereof. You poor son of a bitch, she said. I could tell you a cop I had more fun with. He listened to her about the cop who sang in a patrolmen's glee club. Then he went down into the lobby of the George Cinq and paced a while, trying to decide whether he ought to go back up to that bridal suite and strangle her, or radiogram his lawyers. He radiogrammed his lawyers and the next morning he took the first seat he could get on an Air France stratoliner back to New York. He had tried getting as far away from the Hotel George Cinq as he could. Now, four years later, he was evidently still trying.

Not that he blamed her, he said. He blamed himself. It was his mistake; he had forgotten, temporarily, how rich he was. But not all women were like that, I said. No? he said, polite. I'm not an angel on a wedding cake, I said, but I'm not like that and not all women are like that. He looked at me. He didn't even smile. He just looked tired. I'm sure, he said, my wife would have insisted she was not like that either.

And all this time, she said, we had been talking. I suddenly realized we'd been talking. That he wasn't, any more, a suit of clothes. He wasn't something in a chair. I stopped dancing. I want to sit down, I said. Please. He took me back to the table. You can't do it, can you? he said.

And I couldn't, she said. Not any more. Because I could only do it while I hated him. While I didn't think of him as a man. Or as anything. And I felt so sick. I thought you couldn't, he said. You did your best to look as though you would, but I knew you couldn't. He called the waiter, paid. They were still playing that goddamn tea music. And then he turned. I would like, he said, to see you again, his voice different. He had changed it. No, I said, wanting nothing but to get out of that place, and then I came home, and began to cry, and finally I fell asleep.

Then, later, when she awoke, she felt absurd. That she had cried, that she had been so overwrought, seemed to her ridiculous. Isabel, if she ever told Isabel, would say she was a fool not to have taken the money, a bigger fool to have cried about it, but the biggest fool was Howard: he could have gotten what he wanted for half. And thinking of Isabel, and of Isabel's pearls and Isabel's blondeness, she felt better about it. She was rather glad she hadn't gone through with it; after all, it was hard to believe that really all he'd have asked was to sleep with her, he must have some queerness somewhere; but there was a minute regret, too, that she hadn't. Most of all, now, in the security of her own place, it seemed mildly funny and mildly insane. Life, she was inclined to feel, once more, in that imperishable phrase of hers, was certainly peculiar. She felt quite cheered up now about it all.

And I suppose she actually believed, as she told herself, that she did not want ever to see him again. It was something firm to tell herself, and it did help to re-establish her slightly shaken idea of what she was capable of, and it closed up the tiny abyss which had unexpectedly yawned in her. But she must have known then, with that prescience women have and that skill in reading their own sexual futures, that he would not permit the afternoon to end with so muffled a conclusion; that someday, soon, the telephone would ring again; that flowers would arrive; that a gift, possibly candy, in a larger box than she was used to, or roses, in a cellophane that bore a distinctive florist's address, would be delivered. And have known, too, even while she shuddered a little delicately at the thought that she had come so close to what she called the brink, that the call would be answered, the flowers signed for, the candy accepted.

And I? A queer sort of paralysis seemed to descend on me during the following weeks, as the dinner engagements (all quite innocent, of course) began; the phone calls (pleasant and meaningless and friendly, of course) came; the telegrams (from Denver, where he had flown on business; or Florida, where he had gone for a few days' fishing) were delivered. I would find her now, on the evenings I saw her, unexpectedly animated. She had acquired almost a glow. She looked prettier than ever.

Alfred Hayes

I had almost no knowledge of businessmen, and less of rich
men; I had only supposed that they were different, and that
almost nothing was attractive about them but their money,
and that a girl such as she was, with a taste for music and vague
artistic responses, would necessarily find them bores; nevertheless, as the weeks progressed, I was surprised to discover in
myself other beliefs. Beliefs, for example, hidden away, and as
commonplace as anyone else's, that the penthouses of the city
were inhabited by the mysterious and the fortunate; that,
really, they were an enviable people, the rich; that there, in the
big hotels and the clubs they patronized, life had an unsus-
pected charm; that for them the sun came up over a pleasanter
horizon, and the day began with a purposiveness unknown
elsewhere; that all their mothers were beautiful and cultivated;
and that a floral centerpiece, and a view of the park at night,
made a dinner for two memorable. She, meanwhile, would
laugh at the notion that she was, or could be, attracted to him.
She would repeat to me, then, as we ate dinner, conversations
she had with him, or opinions he voiced. He disliked opera, she
discovered; there was so much singing in it; but he approved of
the ballet; it did have pretty girls, and they danced. Musicals
struck him as what art ought to be; and he was quite violent
about politics. She always had the uncomfortable feeling when
he spoke about the administration in Washington that it was,
in effect, a rival business concern. He played tennis, of course;
and it was not difficult to see him on the tennis courts, in a
T-shirt and white linen shorts, with spotless white woolen
socks and double-soled sneakers, sweating satisfactorily. Or
golf; for there had to be, I was sure, a golf day. Thursday afternoons were the golf afternoons. As for his smaller habits, they
included a cigar cutter attached to a key ring he had a tendency
to toy with, a liking for monograms on his cufflinks and his
shirts, and a particular superstitious affection for a watch

44

inherited from his father, the founder of his business, whom he admired so extravagantly that she asked me if it were possible to have an Oedipus complex about one's father for she had always supposed one had it only about one's mother. She found, too, and this, she said, disturbed her a little, that he had a conviction, more or less absolute, that what he believed was right. He was sure that the judgments he made were the only possible judgments one could make. He felt, she conveyed to me, some identification with the world which she and I lacked. He did not have to fumble (as, listening, I knew I always did) toward what existed. They were his creations, he somehow felt, and he was theirs. A rapport existed between them. What he himself, or his immediate friends, the people on Long Island and between Fifty-ninth Street and Fiftieth, or the oddly mixed set of businessmen, their wives, and (with allowances) the entertainers of the more luxurious cafés, did, he was inclined to think of as normal, acceptable, in short, true. Had he himself been driven to murder, or had it been brought to his attention that one of his acquaintances was living in a menage composed of two women and a young horse, it would not have struck him as unthinkable; he would have nodded his large, well-groomed, dark head to indicate that he understood. Had the two ladies and the young horse been discovered living in a broken-down tenement, that well-groomed head would have gone the other way; the whole episode would then have become incomprehensible.

Nevertheless, she liked him. He was, she discovered, niceish. And kind, despite the experience with the thousand dollars. And quite different, now that she knew him, from what she had supposed. He had, after all, suffered at the hands of women. It was the experience in the George Cinq. She had to admit, in fairness, that it was rather horrible to have a thing like that happen. And naturally, now, she said, frowning, he assumed or had to assume all women were like that, and he was simply trying to guard himself against them; so that, really, he was sort of pathetic when one thought of it. It gave her a pleasant confidence to be able to think of him as sort of pathetic.

And I? Surely there was nothing I could object to; nothing I hadn't myself approved of. Was she flattered by his attention? I could hardly deprive her of the pleasure of that flattery. Was she entertained? I could hardly insist, on the nights I did not see her, that she stay alone in the house, with the little gas pen on the table beside her bed. Then why did I begin to experience that peculiar paralysis? Why was I unaccountably depressed? I had simply to say that I did not want her to see him, or to accept his invitations, and that I loved her, and that I was jealous; nevertheless, I could not. I smiled; I pretended to approve, and pretended not to be alarmed; I entered into the endless comedy of self-concealment with her; and inside me, a slow petrification spread. I seemed incapable of a natural reaction. Was it because, sometimes, listening to her account of him, and of their conversations, and of the evenings they spent together, I saw unexpected resemblances between us, and in his efforts, as a man, to amuse, to impress, to entertain, to dominate and to win her, glimpses of myself? Echoes of what seemed a familiar insincerity came back to me. Or possibly, it was that I, too, found the advantages of knowing a rich man irresistible; that the seductiveness operated equally strong on both of us, and made me, half-willingly, her accomplice.

There was, really, only one incident that broke through for a moment the frozen role I had assigned myself: it was when I found that one of a pair of earrings, of an old silver, which I had given her, was missing. She said, at first, not really wishing to lie, that she had lost the earring; but seeing that I did not believe her, and that I was angry, and that I suspected something, she admitted, with a quick flush, that the earring was now, she guessed, at the bottom of the Hudson River. Which sounded even more unbelievable; but that was where it was, she thought: at the bottom of the river, where he had thrown it one night when they had gone for a drive, and parked, facing the dark Palisades. She had been very fond of the earrings. They were so lovely, and had looked so well with her small head and long neck; they had meant a great deal to her, I knew that, didn't I? She had been absolutely furious with him. I knew that too, didn't I? But there was nothing she could have done; it happened so quickly, so unexpectedly. For they had been sitting in the car, with the radio on, looking at the lights of the amusement park and listening to the music, when he had, without warning, reached toward her and taken the earring from her ear and thrown it toward the river. She supposed it went into the river; she couldn't really see where the ornament had gone; it would have been useless looking for it. She was so mad, and so upset, she almost got out of the Cadillac. But he said he'd rather, when she went out with him, if she was going to wear jewelry, wear his; he was quite willing to buy it for her, too. So that I could see, couldn't I, that there was nothing she could have done about it. She was helpless. The earring was gone, down there in the dark, and he just sat there, undisturbed. He even seemed surprised that she should be so upset about it. He'd send her, he assured her, another pair; and after all, she could understand, couldn't she, his disliking a woman he escorted, or admired, wearing another man's jewelry? His position was perfectly clear; I suspected that she even liked the abruptness with which he had taken something of hers, and disposed of it, easily, quickly, into the darkness. But I understood something else, too: I knew, then, that she had not told him she was in love with me; that, as a matter of fact, she must have allowed him to think there was nobody she was in love with or tied to. The act had been a possessive one; he was throwing away what he thought was a gift from some man she had formerly known; he was, in a way, stripping her of her past. But just as, despite her anger, or the anger she assured me she had felt, and the indignation, she had remained in the car, so I too, because of some not entirely honest feeling, some obscure motive, found myself accepting the act, the disposal of the earring, found myself with an anger that was not entirely genuine, an indignation that something in me was rendering false. But I often saw the gesture repeated: his reaching toward her, and the earring thrown, and the darkness taking it.

So, little by little, she was being absorbed into another life. I suspected, of course, that he must have made a pass of some sort at her; but she denied it. Besides, I knew her better than that; I knew, or I must know, that it was not in her nature to have affairs with two men at identical times; that was, if anything was, the one unforgivable thing. And in addition, she loved me; more than ever, she was certain she loved me; and while she loved me how could she possibly permit another man, no matter how nice, to touch her? Oh, a kiss goodnight perhaps, on a proffered cheek, as she was stepping out of the car; I surely didn't think a goodnight kiss was important? But there were, she explained, things she simply couldn't be guilty of; and I was left to believe, as I was only too anxious to believe, that while she loved me I was safe, and that her relationship with him was simply a convenient one; for, after all, it was nice to go out to a club in the evening, or a smart restaurant, places I could neither afford, nor desired, to take her; I'd be so bored at places like that, she assured me; knowing me, she knew how bored I'd be.

So there were evenings when they drove to Long Island, to one of the gambling casinos on the Point; evenings when they were invited to dinner at some friend's in the East Fifties. She found his friends not quite so stuffy as she had thought they would be. And she found, too, that they were taken with her. She looked so modest, tender, young, innocent; and yet she had a child, and yet she had been married; she gave off, for them, her own little aura of pathos. She aroused little currents of sympathy. She dressed simply; she arrived without a mink coat; she wasn't blonde; she had good manners; she could be prevailed upon to play the piano and to sing. She began to see that he was pleased with the impression she made upon his friends. And then, she had a quick childish enthusiasm: when the curtain at a musical was about to rise, when the lights came down and the orchestra vamped into the opening bars of the overture, she seemed about to clap her hands, her eyes sparkled, a charming spontaneity took possession of her; and that pleased him, too; that he could take her to the theater and see the evidence of her delight in being taken. She, on her part, made her own constant revisions about him. She began to see him as less boring than solid. When he spoke of his family, she discerned in him a strong devotion to the idea of a home, of children, of an interrelated social unit. She realized that he was less frightening than she supposed. She began to lose some of the intimidation she had felt about his money. She was very careful, too, not to accept gifts that were too large. He had offered many times to exchange the shabby fur she wore, and which she claimed to be so attached to, for something more presentable in at least beaver, but she resisted his kindness and continued to wear the fur, which continued to shed, and as it shed continued to bring to the mouths of the wives of the friends whose expensive flats they dined at curiously sympathetic and knowing smiles.

I think that, in losing her, for it was inevitable that I should lose her, what bothered me most was that I lost her to somebody I could not feel superior to; that, secretly, the bristling idea of his money had intimidated me too. I suppose if she had simply left me and there had been a temporary vacuum, a decent space her devotion to knitting or a trip to Chicago had filled, I might not have behaved as I did. It was, of course, silly of me to assume that she wouldn't have, when the time came, provided herself with a more than adequate replacement, for it is hardly natural for a woman to dispose of a man until accident or design has already provided her with the promise of another. For a while, I imagine, she was torn; before she could make a decision of any kind she had to be sure. There must have been a moment, therefore, a sign of a special kind, an expression of a distinct sort of concern on his part (a night she had been unhappy, and had cried, and he had comforted her; an unusual pressure upon her hand as they said good-by; a revealing tenderness in his voice as he asked if she had a headache) that had convinced her she could at last be sure. Of course a woman always seems to choose, with a dismaying instinct, the goddamnedest moments to end a love affair. Her dismissals always seem to come the way assassinations do, from the least expected quarter. There will be a note on the kitchen table, propped up against the sugar bowl, on exactly the day when most in love with her you arrive carrying a cellophaned orchid; or walking along the avenue, one arm about her waist, and talking with great enthusiasm about a small house you saw for sale cheap thirty minutes from New York. They seem timed to arrive during birthday parties, when you are apparently happiest, or relaxing in a hot bath, when the house is most peaceful, or taking a short walk in the garden, enjoying what promises to be a beautiful evening. She waits until that precise moment you are bending down to sniff the roses, and thinking that, after all, she is a wonderful girl, and you are really absolutely sold on her, and that the life between you has been, for all the small quarrels and differences, really fine,

when bang: she fires from behind the rosebush. Her own particular shot was discharged on an evening when I was having
dinner, the classic quiet one, with a friend, at a small Italian
restaurant downtown, which had a back yard over which an
awning had been stretched. A dozen tables were set out on the
cement floor, and the walls of the tenements of the neighborhood reared up on all sides. A mechanical fan stirred the heavy
late summer air; a spiral of flypaper hung from one of the iron
props of the awning, and twirled, with its bag of dead flies,
slowly in the wind the fan made. An elderly waiter, in a short-
sleeved white shirt, with a spotted black cummerbund, sweated
his way from the kitchen to the tables, carrying the steaming
plates of spaghetti and lasagna. It was a setting beautifully
arranged: shabby, peaceful, deceptive. It required only that I
should be in the act of reaching for the bread in the bread
basket; that I should nod, a bit surprised, when George men-
tioned that she had telephoned him earlier in the evening;
that I should explain, with a rather fatuous pleasure, that I was
going to meet her later; that I should turn as the waiter
approached, and that George should say: But she doesn't want
to meet you later. Then it required only that I should hesi-
tate, that I should not believe I had heard what I heard, that I
should believe that what she had said on the phone was that
she had been delayed and wanted to see me at a later time, and
that George should look uncomfortable, even a bit pitying,
since he was the unlucky transmitter, and repeat to me again
that no, I didn't understand, that wasn't what she meant; to be
exact, then, as though the message had come in code and had
to be accurately translated by the experts on messages in that
cipher, men of long experience, trustworthy too, and to say
that the message meant she did not want ever to see me, not
that night and not any night. Not ever again: that was the exact
translation.

When I looked at the tenements, now, and at the windows from which clotheslines were strung, and in which women, stout and thick-armed, in chemises, moved between the kitchen tables and the stoves; or looked at the sky, darkening now, and pinched between the roofs; a sky neither distant nor near; or stared again at the tablecloth on the table, stained with wine or stained with sauce, it seemed to me as though something had shifted, or been violently moved, for everything, in those few moments after I understood what the message really meant, appeared to be in a different focus, to be at once clearer and emptier than I remembered it. Everything seemed abruptly sharper than before, and duller, as though something had been in those few minutes drained out from the world to which I was accustomed. I was, apparently, shaken, who had never expected himself to be shaken. But then anger came to steady the bad pitch of my voice. To have it end like this! With a telephone call, and a spiral of flypaper slowly turning. With a message she had not had the courage to deliver herself. With so dull a thud, and so lame a conclusion. I had always assumed that when it ended it would end with a certain gracefulness, a sad and thoughtful charm, a tender farewell. But there were only the dead flies, here, and the blank tenements, and the elderly waiter. She had deprived me of an exit I had planned a long time, and carefully. Then it seemed to me I was being badly treated. God, the days I'd worried about her! The concern I had displayed! For she was, I saw now, quite capable of taking care of herself; and I, who had postponed for so long a time the decision to leave her, who had (I thought) been so careful of her feelings, so reluctant (I thought) to hurt her, so solicitous (I thought) of her welfare, had been the one to be shunted aside with so little consideration. Well, I was quite sure, now, that I was glad it was over; I was free again. There was a surge of possibility, a brief (and illusory) sense of well-being. Then, abruptly, I was dispirited, and wanted to be alone.

I left the restaurant, passing the hot kitchen, where the woman who owned the place cooked, a cheerful woman in an apron, who nodded to me as she nodded to all the departing customers. It was now close to ten o'clock. A wind had sprung up. I began to walk toward Fifth Avenue.

5

Oddly enough, I continued to believe that she had not gone to bed with him.

I had been in the way, and she had dispensed with me. It was a bitter enough fact to accept. The sense of well-being which had flooded through me as I sat at the table and thought of not having now the burden of another's life on me had almost entirely vanished, and the humiliation of the choice she had made, and the quickness with which she had discarded me, had deepened. There were the beginnings of an unfamiliar anguish inside me now. I told myself, of course, that she was not worth even the small suffering I was beginning to experience, and that, finally, now that I could see it in perspective, the long year together had been largely waste. But the suffering, if it was suffering, for I was not yet sure that I was suffering, continued on its own ambiguous level.

In the park there were moths whirling within the circle of the lights of the street lamps, and there were old men still playing checkers in the difficult light. I turned uptown.

Did I want her? I thought to myself. Suppose, now, she were to change her mind: did I want her? Of course not, I assured myself. Was her loss important? How stupid to imagine it was. Nothing of any significance had happened. It was simply that my own life was so barren, or seemed so barren; the temporary possession of her had given me the illusion that it was not, while I had her, barren; now that she was gone, the barrenness that she had temporarily helped conceal lay exposed. It was because we thought so much that love could save us, that having nothing else but the dry labor of our work we looked so anxiously toward love. It was our ridiculous phoenix. Somebody had reported that its nest had been discovered. We were waiting for the apparition, for the feathered resurrection, for the bird of endless hope with the imperishable plumage, quite sure the bird did not exist, eager for the slightest rumor it did. To suffer, or to experience a suffering for the loss of a girl who had no importance, was absurd; I was absurd because I was suffering; it was something that required hiding away because of its absurdity.

It was becoming painful to think. There seemed to be inside me whole areas I had to be careful of. I could feel my mind, like a paw, wince away from certain sharp recollections. I contained, evidently, a number of wounded ideas.

So, with the only face I had, I continued to walk uptown, imitating a man who is out for some air or a little exercise before bed.

Had I lost her because of cowardice? Because of too little desire? Was I unable to hold or possess anyone?

Sad and preposterous, I thought. It seemed to me that was what I was most: sad and preposterous. It was not that I had been happy with her; I was quite sure I had not been happy. But there were images of her which turned stiffly in my mind as though they were little lead figures attached to a mechanism: images of her on the green daybed, images of her combing her hair. I knew that she had wanted what I was not prepared to give her: the illusion that she was safe, the idea she was protected. She had expected, being beautiful, the rewards of being beautiful; at least some of them; one wasn't beautiful for nothing in a world which insisted that the most important thing for a girl to be was beautiful. Perhaps now, I thought, she would have some of the things she imagined she wanted: the cocker spaniel, the nursery with the wallpaper that had little sailing boats on it and flying fish, the lawn with an automatic sprinkler, and somebody else to do the dishes. And it wasn't only the money. Possibly the money was not so important to her as I contemptuously told myself it was. She was tired. At twenty-two she was tired. They tired young nowadays. They were willing to call it quits at twenty-two. She had been a little too young for me, and a little too desperate. Women in their blossoming thirties were better for what I wanted women for; a little more experienced, a little less intense; women for whom a love affair wasn't any longer so desperate an enterprise. What there was of it, I told myself, I'd had; what I was entitled to I'd got; I'd never get more, being the man I was, and living the life I'd chosen for myself.

A clock in a jeweler's window said eleven. I had walked all the way uptown. I was again at that familiar corner with its subway kiosk, her tenement with the bar and grill on the street level, her delicatessen with its imported groceries, the great bulk of her office building. I looked up: the windows were dark. She was still not home; or was she home?

Once around the block, I thought. Give her until midnight.

In the bar and grill, there was a communal shabbiness of a sort. The customers ranged along the bar, almost looking as though they knew each other, almost looking as though they were there together. You ought to get drunk, I said; at least that would be a place to be, the bar. But you can't, I said; you get ill, you know that, it's your stomach, you can't get drunk even if you want to. I really didn't have a good vice. Liquor in moderate quantities. Love on the installment plan. Wouldn't it be nice if I could really cultivate some impressive vice? Some excessive cruelty or some astonishing sacrifice. But not even that. Instead, we complain in small voices. Complain we've married the wrong girl, taken the wrong job, lived the wrong lives.

And what pitiful attempts we make at cures: we raise vegetables in ridiculous gardens, we apply for membership in athletic clubs, we promise ourselves to read again all the important books we've neglected. We think that what we want is a simpler life, and a more active, a more external one, and every Wednesday we diligently attend the square dances at the local schoolhouse imagining that a Virginia reel is the way back into a friendly community, and that denims and a checked shirt will restore communication with the stranger who lives next door.

The only thing we haven't lost, I thought, is the ability to suffer. We're fine at suffering. But it's such a noiseless suffering. We never disturb the neighbors with it. We collapse, but we collapse in the most disciplined way. That's us. That's certainly us. The disciplined collapsers.

Suicide quietly with sleeping pills in a tiled bath. Neat gassings in a duplex. No trouble to anyone; the will notarized and the floor swept and the telephone on its hook.

Your only vice, I thought, is yourself. The worst of all. The really incurable one.

It was twelve o'clock. There was a light in the windows. I went into the bar. As I went toward the telephone booth, the phone rang. I answered it. It was somebody wanting somebody named Eddie Cohen. I said to the bartender: Is there somebody here named Eddie Cohen?

The bartender called: Eddie Cohen here?

There was no Eddie Cohen.

I told whoever it was at the other end of the phone that there was no Eddie Cohen. He's there every night, the voice said, and then hung up. I dialed her number.

6

The door opened cautiously on its length of chain, and one eye, the eye of my favorite Cyclops, regarded me.

Are you drunk? she said. You smell drunk, not knowing whether she should open the door or risk my making a disturbance there in the hall. She thought she knew me well enough to suppose that if she did not open the door I would make a disturbance. The possibility of my making one was enough, for I had acquired somehow the reputation of being occasionally violent, and she did not want that sort of a scandal, with me knocking at the bolted door, and all the neighbors out in the hallway, and somebody perhaps going for the police. I looked to her, I suppose, through the narrow aperture, bleak enough at that moment to seem capable of assaulting her door knob; but I wouldn't have. Had she closed the door firmly, had she threatened to telephone the police, stiff with a ridiculous contempt for her I'd have turned and descended the dirty stairs again. For I was not the lover who strangled her; I was not the demented pounder on doors. She knew me badly, really. She overestimated the violence in me. She took the chain off, and opened the door.

I looked quickly over the living room; the bed was not disturbed. She wore a skirt and a high turtle-neck black sweater. She had evidently just come into the house. I had intended to be cold, but somewhere a pulse was beating away uncontrollably.

Why didn't you wait until tomorrow to tell me? I said.

What difference would one day have made? she answered.

And what difference would it? I knew, too, in that common knowledge we shared, that we had come to the end of it; that nothing, the delay of a day, kisses or going to bed again, would have changed it; nevertheless, it seemed to me that I would have had some mysterious satisfaction and would have accepted it more easily if we had, this one final night, gone to bed together. It seemed to me that this was all I wanted, and that it was not too much to have asked or expected. My bitterness seemed all based on the fact that I had been deprived of that very final night. Her face, the room itself, its details, the bed covered and against the wall, pressed on me with an intolerable weight. The pulse continued to pound; I was aware of my hands, how hot they were, and dry.

Now she was searching my face anxiously to see how agitated I was, and what it was I intended to do. She did not believe that I would hurt her, and yet she was afraid that I might hurt her. But she was in no danger. She would have been struck by nothing heavier than a laborious adjective. She was quite safe, and needed only to have permitted me to exhaust the not very effective phrases with which I clumsily tried to transfix her, and to empty myself of all the exaggerated accusations I made against her, and have allowed me to drain the cisterns of self-pity, and I would have turned, satisfied, and have made, or tried to make, an exit appropriate to the moment: the door theatrically slammed, and my footsteps going loudly down the stairs. She should have, had she been penetrating enough, even permitted me the luxury of a bitter and conclusive: whore.

I had said now all the outrageous things I could summon up; drawn for her that picture of myself waiting anxiously for midnight, huddled in a doorway on a dark street, wanting to be with her, waiting for the light to appear in her window; how

I had been, particularly today, so much in love with her; how I had thought, at last, that what was wrong between us would be finally straightened out; how shocked I'd been to hear from someone else the decision that she had not had the simple courage to give to me herself; how she had owed me at least that. Were there tears now in my eyes? I had conjured them up. How satisfactory their warm salt tasted on my mouth. She could not disbelieve the tears.

And with the tears, softening, she said: Oh, darling, I couldn't tell you. If I saw your face, if I had to look at you, while I told you, I wouldn't have been able to do it. You know I couldn't look at your face and tell you. I did the only thing I could, the only way I could, darling, darling.

(For I had crossed, suddenly, to where she sat on the edge of the bed, and put my head in her lap.)

Why did you drink? she said. You shouldn't drink. And you mustn't call me. It has to be over. (How reassuring to lie, like this, in a pretense of utter defeat and complete helplessness, in the comfort of her lap.) Were you really, she said, stroking my head, standing out there all this time, waiting? How terrible. Suppose there were someone here? You'd hurt yourself more. It's better like this, you know that. I couldn't go on, just drifting. I don't know who I am any more, or where I'm going. And I loved you. Truly, believe me, I loved you. No matter what you think now. It's because of Barbara. And it wouldn't have worked out, you know that, darling, and I have to be practical, I have to think of my future. And muffled in her lap, the tear-stained voice that was hardly mine agreed that yes perhaps it was better this way, the way she had chosen, and we would avoid the delayed farewell, the protracted departure, the postponed break-up. For she had, she said, to comfort me, not wished to cause me any pain. I was dear to her, and she would not, if it were at all possible, cause me any pain. And I'd forgive her, because I understood how it was, what necessities drove her. I would forgive her, here, now, this final time we were to see each other, this tear-swept moment, as we drew apart, dividing from each other. What was I to forgive her for? Oh, everything. For everything was wrong; everything needed forgiving. I embraced her; fiercely. As though to add to all the ancient embraces this last unforgettable one. This one that would endure in memory. This imperishable clasp. For already I thought of her as ghostly. Her eyes acquired a sympathetic mist. Her small childish mouth, endeavoring to be firm, trembled in the bittersweet drama. And so, holding her, this, which was to be the last of all our kisses, crawled from her cheek to the small ear, then to her throat. She moved in my arms; frightened, almost. And I imagined it was because she did not wish to respond to me; that to feel desire now would be almost a violation of the very tender membrane of emotion that was stretched between us. But I'd kissed her there so often. It was where she was most vulnerable. A delicate shudder always went through her when my mouth touched her lightly there. I could taste the rough wool of her sweater now, and reaching up, thinking perhaps I could revive some ghost of passion in her, I slid the sweater down on her throat, and she cried, no! no! Embedded there, where I had moved the sweater, were the swollen and purple markings of teeth.

She was out of my arms, and there I was, stupidly on my knees, staring at her. My mouth worked; I made some unfinished gesture with my hand. He hadn't, after all, needed the thousand dollars. She was trying quite hard not to appear frightened. It was why she had worn the sweater. I said: not a cat. Not a cat at all. A little mouse in heat. I got up from the floor where I had been kneeling. I think that I had been kneeling made it worse. I said: You powdered it, didn't you? You put cold cream on it. It didn't help. There's only one position a man can get himself into to achieve a bite like that. I mimicked her voice. I repeated her denials. He had only kissed her, a tender good night. I said: Why bother to cover it up? One on the other side would make a nice pair.

She had started to scream.

It was stupid to scream. I wasn't going to kill her. Not exactly.

Besides, she should have been beaten. A little. I think that would have been just: to beat her, a little.

Halfway across the room, she picked up the teargas pen, and fired it.

7

A few days later, there was a disturbance down the corridor. Mr Lanzetti, a round man, who was the hotel's assistant manager, explained when I opened my door that it was a woman. The occupant of 615 had thrown her out.

She was outside 615 now, kicking at the door. She was red-haired.

You son of a bitch, she shouted at 615, you'll pay for this.

Mr Lanzetti fluttered to her.

Madame, Mr Lanzetti said, you'll just force me to call the police. Is that what you want, I should call the police?

Shut up, the red-haired woman said. Fatface.

All right then, Mr Lanzetti said. Bob.

Yes sir, the elevator boy said.

Telephone the police.

The police, the red-haired woman said. She slung her purse which she wore on a shoulder strap out of the way. Go call the sucking police. I'll cut your balls off, she shouted at the locked door.

The door of 615 remained wisely closed.

Madame, Mr Lanzetti said. You're just making a spectacle of yourself. You're just disturbing our tenants.

Screw your tenants, the red-haired woman said. Throw me out. He's got another guess coming if he thinks he can just lay me and throw me out. I don't go that easy. I'll cut his

63

balls off. So help me Mary. Sidney! she screamed. Open this door!

Madame, Mr Lanzetti said.

Madame your ass, the red-haired woman said. She began methodically to kick again at Sidney's door.

Then someone called the police and they took the lady away.

So that others and elsewhere were having difficulties with love. Madame your ass. She was quite right, the lady in the corridor. I wished that I too, having been betrayed, could kick at the door of outrage. That I could howl somewhere in an empty corridor. I closed my own door, wondering if Sidney had ever had a teargas pen fired at him.

I was sleeping badly. In the mornings I would awaken from some dream in which, again, I had lost something, and would again, with great anxiety and rage, try to recover it. She wore, in one dream I had, a red beret. It was raining. I followed her in the rain and called to her. Apparently she didn't hear me. She walked rapidly away and then disappeared into a penny arcade. I remembered that the bus she took had a terminal behind such an arcade. There were men standing at the pinball machines and the various games under hot lights. I looked for her where the mechanical gypsy read fortunes. I had lost her somewhere among the intent and unlucky players. When I woke up I could remember very distinctly how she had looked in the red beret hurrying away in the rain.

I made spasmodic efforts to work, assuring myself that once I began working I would forget her. The difficulty was in beginning. There was a feeling of weakness, a sort of powerlessness now, as though I were about to be ill but was never quite ill enough, as though I were about to come down with something I did not quite come down with. It seemed to me that for the first time in my life I had been in love, and had lost, because of the grudgingness of my heart, the possibility of having what, too late, I now thought I wanted. What was it that all my life I had so carefully guarded myself against? What was it that I had felt so threatened me? My suffering, which seemed to me to be a strict consequence of having guarded myself so long, appeared to me as a kind of punishment, and this moment, which I was now enduring, as something which had been delayed for half a lifetime. I was experiencing, apparently, an obscure crisis of some kind. My world acquired a tendency to crumble as easily as a soda cracker. I found myself horribly susceptible to small animals, ribbons in the hair of little girls, songs played late at night over lonely radios. It became particularly dangerous for me to go near movies in which crippled girls were healed by the unselfish love of impoverished bellhops. I had become excessively tender to all the more obvious evidences of the frailness of existence; I was capable of dissolving at the least kind word, and self-pity, in inexhaustible doses, lay close to my outraged surface. I moved painfully, an ambulatory case, mysteriously injured.

I began, too, to experience the conceit of suffering. It conferred upon me a significance my emotions had previously lacked. It seemed a special destiny. Because I suffered I thought I loved, for the suffering was the proof, the testimony of a heart I had suspected was dry. Since happiness had failed me, it was unhappiness that provided me with the belief that I was, or had been, in love, for it was easier to believe in the reality of unhappiness when I had before me the evidence of sleepless nights and the bitterness of reaching in the dark for what was no longer there. The sick constriction of the heart was undeniable; there was a melancholy truth in the fact that it was suffering which made me, I thought, at last real to myself.

There were times when I would forget her, though they were rare, and it would be for a time as though she had never existed; and then some passing girl's inadvertent gesture, or an accidental profile, or a hat like hers, would restore her, and restore the suffering too, and I would long again, somehow, to encounter or to see her. I would recall her melancholias. I would recall how she would say: don't look at me when I put my lipstick on, for it made her nervous. How there was always something she had just lost or just misplaced, and the desperation with which she would dig into the cluttered depths of her purse. How it always required persuasion to have her wear boots on a rainy day. And the fear of age. How she thought her prettiness would go and how she saw herself withered at thirty-five. Now she had passed into another life. She inhabited a world from which I was excluded, and she had left me in an immense empty space.

The world she inhabited now was one which I, privately, thought of as superior to my own, and I would expect sometimes, when I passed under the canopies of the big clubs, with their uniformed doormen, that I might encounter her, or as the dark powerful cars swung into the curb that perhaps she would be issuing from a vehicle like that. My failure to hold her was simply one more of the failures I had to endure in the struggle with that world, and I really should not have expected a victory. That she should have finally chosen that life, the life those powerfully hooded cars and the canopies and the uniformed doormen represented, seemed to me now inevitable. It contained all the attractions; it held all the promises. I supposed that by now the violent markings of his teeth had vanished, and she was again wearing her usual dresses.

She spoke to George, whom she thought of as a friend, once a week or so, over the phone, and she seemed happy, at least she seemed happy over the phone; she had spent the weekend horseback riding, and it had been fun; or she would mention, George said, openly now, a friend of Howard's who had a plane, and she was going to learn to fly it; or she would be on the phone, yawning, because they'd been out so late the night before. She slept later than ever, as the last pretenses of work fell away from her, and she told George that she had had Howard drive her home one weekend and she introduced him, quite formally, as she supposed she should, to her family. It must have been quite an occasion, I thought, when the big Cadillac had pulled up on the quiet shady street and she had gotten out of it. Barbara had liked him, she said, and George said that she was obviously preparing herself and him and everybody else for the announcement of a marriage, or at least an engagement. Of course he hadn't said yet, she told George, anything definite, she did not want him to feel she was rushing anything, but she was quite sure that in time he would come to it. He was going away for a few days to Utah: there was a mine he had bought into, and they had found, in addition to the lead and silver, a vein of gold or something, she wasn't quite sure, and she thought that when he came back she would speak to him. I could tell from what George said that she felt reasonably confident now, and that she had secured herself enough with him to think that it was only a question of time. It was true that they had had an argument or so, now and then, but it was not important. She told George what the argument was, and I suppose she told her other friend, Vivian, too. He had been reading the late paper, sitting in his big living room, and she had been in a chair, opposite, eating an apple and glancing through a copy of *Vogue*, when he said: They're floating the Big Mo. She said: What? He said: They're floating the Big Mo. She said: What in God's name is the Big Mo? He said: Don't you read the papers? She said: Well how am I supposed to know what the Big Mo is? Is it a gangster? So he'd been mad, and then she had gotten mad at him, with his old papers, because it was true that she never did look at the front page, after all there was almost nothing on it that concerned her, and she told him he was opinionated, that he never thought anybody was right but himself, which he'd taken offense at, so that it had been a bad evening, but he'd called in the morning and apologized and she, to show him that she forgave him, promised she'd look at the front page after that so at least they'd have something to talk about. But she told George that both of them had been so angry she had forgotten to ask what the Big Mo was, and George had to tell her.

Meanwhile, I continued to endure as best I could the silence of my own living room, the emptiness of my own bed. I thought, intermittently, of leaving town; a trip would be good, George advised me, and I had wanted for some time to see Bermuda. I did go so far as to collect the travel folders and ask about the fare and the accommodations, and to think about how it would be walking through Hamilton, looking at the policemen in their khaki shorts and sun helmets, but the enormous lethargy which chained me to my sofa would not release me, and I did not go to Bermuda or anyplace. I did go one night to a house on Riverside Drive. There were four gentlemen in the living room, which was sunken and very nicely rugged, playing gin rummy in their shirt sleeves, and there was a large multiknobbed blond television set which was broadcasting the fights at St Nick's and now and then one of the gin rummy players would turn away from the game which was being played for a dollar a point and look with a not entirely interested eye at the boxers, and then turn back for the next deal. In the kitchen I could see there had been arranged, or a caterer had arranged, neat stacks of corned beef sandwiches, a green hill of dill pickles, and a dozen or so bottles of celery tonic. In the bedroom, which was just off the foyer, there were two girls posing on a pair of twin beds while a photographer took flashlight pictures of them. An elderly smiling gentleman in black and white sport shoes and a forty-dollar pair of gabardine

slacks was admiring, as I glanced in, the two girls, one of whom
was a large blonde and entirely naked, and the other a thin
dark Spanish girl who wore still her black lace panties which
had little red bows on them, and they were both smiling for the
camera, and possibly also for the elderly gentleman who was
being very helpful with the flashbulb apparatus. You could
smell the spiced odor of the corned beef all the way into the
bedroom. I went down the two steps into the sunken living
room to watch for a while the gin rummy game and the fights
at St Nick's. In a little while the elderly gentleman appeared,
his shoelaces untied. Is there any cherry soda? he said. She
wants cherry soda. He disappeared into the kitchen, smiling, I
thought, more than ever. I left the living room when even a
dollar a point did not make gin rummy a game you could
watch very long, and entered what I suppose the host sometimes called a den and sometimes a library, but which was, I
could see, the really fascinating room in the apartment, much
more than either the living room or the bedroom, though of
course they were fascinating too, but not quite in the way the
library-den was. For while it contained a few Book of the
Month Club books, its most striking feature was a powerful
telescope on a tripod eternally pointing its eye through the
Venetian blinds toward the bedrooms of the city. The telescope
was, naturally, adjustable, and must have been a lot of fun, and
I suppose the people who used it often thought of how really
entertaining it could be if there were a sound track attached. I
used the telescope for a while but there was nothing really happening anywhere, and then I discovered the stereopticon,
which was three-dimensional, and the cases of colored slides,
and I spent twenty-five minutes dropping the slides into the
viewer looking at what must have been a considerable part of
the female population of New York. I had no idea there were so
many girls in the business. I remember trying to find some

relationship other than statistical between the inexhaustible nakedness of the girls on their tiger skins and beside their pools and on the equally inexhaustible beds and what was causing me so constant and inescapable a suffering. I was sure that there had to be a connection of a kind, for how vast could the possible difference be between what my eye, fixed to the viewer, saw, and what my mind, fixed to her image, imagined? The difference could not be in the tiger skins and the illuminated swimming pools, and there was not, really, enough anatomical distinction to make a point about. I felt as though I were close to some important and possibly influential discovery, but I never made it. The door of the bedroom was discreetly closed as I left the apartment, but I thought I could understand why, now, the gin rummy game absorbed the players so.

So there was that night, and another night when I did get drunk enough, and ill enough, to injure myself and woke up in the morning with two great inexplicable bruises on my ribs, and I remembered, after trying to recall where it was and how it was I had gotten them, that I had been in and out all night of telephone booths, ringing her, and that there had been no answer for which, now, sober and exhausted, I was rather glad. I had by now come to accept the state in which I was, the inertia and the dull suffering and the endless and useless recollections of her, and the endless thinking of how it would have been different had I done this or done that, and the alternations of an almost unbearable desire to see her with a hatred which seemed about to free me of her but then didn't. Everybody, of course, assured me that I would recover. It was an illness each had, in his own way, they privately admitted, lived through, and had called the usual doctors about, and taken to the nearest drugstore the usual prescriptions, and they knew that I, too, would find myself one morning a well man again. Nothing, evidently, healed with such certainty as a broken heart; and even if the heart was not broken, as I was convinced that it was impossible mine was, but simply dislocated a little, there were infallible remedies of which the most infallible was time. Meanwhile, there were recommendations, advice, telephone numbers, little dinners arranged with myself solicitously placed between some sympathetic married couple, long walks in the park, insomnia. That morning when I would awake and find the pillows not lumpish nor the sheets twisted like nooses seemed still immeasurably distant. My greatest difficulty appeared to be that I could not determine in my own mind, with any certainty, what it was I myself felt about her. She escaped me; even now, after all that had happened between us, she escaped me. Did I actually believe that only the possession of that particular body, the act of kissing again those particular breasts and lying again close to those particular thighs, would ease this agony I was enduring? I thought of myself as I had been with her: delivering flowers, like an errand boy; kissing her, like an actor; tormenting her, like a villain; consoling her, like a doctor; advising her, like a lawyer; and they were all, all, somehow comic, somehow unbelievable, gestures hardly mine. It was impossible to understand! I was in the midst of ridiculous mysteries, great enigmas of need and bulking sphinxes of necessity. All I knew, really, was that she had taken away with her when she had gone something which in the past had held me together, some necessary sense of myself, something without which I seemed in danger of collapsing; and whatever it was, an indispensable vanity, an irreplaceable idea of my own invulnerability, it was gone and only she could restore it to me, or so I thought. For without whatever it was, I seemed poor, depleted, injured in some mysterious way; without it, there was nothing to interpose between the world and me. And now, more than ever, as the weeks went by, she seemed lost forever. My cowardice, my reluctance to declare myself, my habitual irony, myself in short as the years had made me, had lost her. How intolerable now the weight of what I was seemed upon me. How subtle a punishment life had devised. Often I felt as though my own pain had cornered me in some room and I was alone with it, like some animal that was inescapable. It was a terrifying experience to find oneself at last helpless, and to be made helpless by something for which one could not, anywhere, ask help. But when we have suffered long enough we adjust to the idea finally that we have always suffered, and that it was never any different, and a mock sort of health is eventually achieved. The suffering having endured so long seems at last through the simplicities of repetition to be less intense; we learn to move, in our crippled way, quite well, and one would hardly notice, if they were strangers, the difference the infirmity has made. We lower to the level of the wound, and begin to think we are fine again, as I began to think, and begin almost to find the world a less inimical place, as I began to find it, when late one night, after I had gone to bed, and was lying in the darkness, nearly asleep, she telephoned. It was about three o'clock in the morning. I had been reading and I had just turned the light off when the phone rang. There was a small humble diffident voice at the other end of the line that I almost did not recognize as hers; and then my heart gave a great swift bound. Cleopatra, I said. Are you alone? she asked, in that excessively humble voice, as though she had forfeited the right to call me at three o'clock in the morning, and if I were to hang up now abruptly it would be a fate she justly deserved. Alone? I said, no, Mark Antony was with me, we'd been reading together, a book on asps; and then I was tired of talking like that. I suspected that, for a moment, so concentrated was she on the decision to call me, she had almost thought Mark Antony really was someone I might possibly be with, because she said, to reassure herself: But you are alone, aren't you? She, too, was alone; she, too, was lying in the darkness. She had not been able to sleep, and the voice diminished itself diffidently: she had been thinking of me. My heart gave another of its quick immense bounds. She had said just enough and said it in such a way that I knew something had happened between her and Howard. She would like, she said, to see me; tomorrow, perhaps, if of course I weren't busy, at lunch, as though lunch were all she dared hope for; but tomorrow and lunch were too distantly away. I would not, I knew, though perhaps it would be wiser, be able to endure the long intermission until tomorrow; no, I'd come now. Will you really? she said, the voice eager and the eagerness flattering, as though I had promised to do the one great thing she had wished most for and had not dared ask; and I said yes, as quickly as getting dressed and a taxi could do it. Hurry, hurry, she said.

Twenty minutes later, there I was again, climbing those stairs I had not climbed in three months, noting how nothing had changed: that while I had suffered, her world had remained exactly as it had always been. This time the chain came off the door instantly when I knocked; and there she was, wearing (she had, I thought, put it on almost as soon as I had said I would be over) the knee-length terrycloth bathrobe, and smoking, which she did rarely, a cigarette. I supposed she had rearranged whatever in the room needed rearranging. But I was seeing her; she was there, before me, real after all the phantoms of her I had conjured up: the imagined girls walking on the avenue who had resembled her, the girls talking animatedly in the front seats of Cadillacs who had had hair like hers, the girls I had expected to come issuing out of the doors that doormen held of night clubs. The smile she gave me trembled hesitantly on her mouth, a smile unsure of itself and asking to be reassured, a smile that was to take the place of all the words she did not trust and which might possibly betray her.

I supposed she had prepared herself for all my possible reproaches; I supposed she had prepared, while I was dressing, those explanations she thought absolutely necessary. I had thought, too, that I would demand explanations, and that her telephoning me had given me an advantage I should not easily relinquish; that whatever it was that had happened between them, I would be cautious; but now as I entered the small familiar room, and she stood there, not even quite as beautiful as I had remembered her, her face cleansed and shining a little with cream, and the cigarette being awkwardly smoked, something welled up in me and broke, like a great bubble, and there, once more, I was kneeling before her, my arms encircling her small waist, my head against the warmth of her belly, wanting nothing but an interminable silence in which all my longing for her would be at last satisfied. She seemed as deeply moved as I was, as though only this inarticulateness could express the depth of feeling our absence from each other had created. I felt as though I had been starved for her; my hands told, or tried to tell her, the sort of hunger I had endured; the muteness of my arms about her, and my face buried in the cloth of her robe struggled dumbly to convey to her all the desperation of those nights in which, wanting her, I had not had her: dumbly, in a pantomime of longing. Had I been arrogant? Then, here, kneeling before her, I was no longer arrogant. The scorn which I had so often expressed for those men who became absolutely dependent on women had been put off, and kneeling so I wanted her to believe now that only a vast and inexpressible need for her existed, and that this submission was my repentance for all the doubts I had ever wittily or stupidly declared about my love for her. Possibly she had told herself that if I were cold, or too obviously triumphant, or nasty, when I came to the house, she would not endure it, or she would endure only a little of it, enough to show her own sincere desire to be reconciled, and had convinced herself that, really, all she was doing in telephoning me was giving both of us another chance. I supposed, if that was what she had thought or expected, the completeness with which I had knelt, and the long expressive silence, had convinced her that she was in no danger of having to endure my gloating over her. We were lying now, finally, together on the bed; the urgency had at last subsided. It had been terrible, she said, her voice low and her face averted, it had been terrible for her too; there had been so many times she had expected to encounter me as I had expected to encounter her: and with another girl. Hadn't there really been another girl? Not that she would have minded; she would have understood, perfectly, she said, if some night I had taken another girl to bed, for she, too, had been persuaded every-thing was over. She had thought she had seen me once, riding a bus, and she had had such an awful pang; she had not thought, either, that she would suffer as much as she had. Of course, she had gone out, every evening as a matter of fact, but the going out made it easier, a little easier, because there were so many memories embedded in this room, and besides, in Howard's set they went out every evening, it was just unthinkable stay-ing home one night. To have stayed home would have been to admit that life was not quite so fascinating in the places they went to as everybody pretended it was, and there was really nothing to do, she said, for them but to spend money, and she had gotten so tired of that, all the spending. Nevertheless, that could hardly have convinced her, I thought, to break up with Howard; it would have required something more severe than her being tired, or even a little bored, if she had really been bored, for I remembered the horseback riding and the plane she was going to learn to fly. No, no; she really had been bored, utterly bored, even though the horseback riding had been fun, and she had never really gotten to the plane, it was only something the friend had promised her. She had been bored because the realization came to her, finally, how alien to her the sort of life he led really was; and there were so many differences between them, what he liked and asked out of life, and what she liked and asked out of life; and it had come to her most sharply one night when Isabel said to her: It's so funny, I see you and Howard together, and you hold hands, and he calls you darling and you call him dear, and yet it's as though you were perfect strangers. Isabel had been, because she was fond of her, and worried about her, frank; and then it presented itself to her as being so absolutely true: she did feel like a perfect stranger, despite the darlings and the dears, and they would always be, she realized with an awful suddenness, perfect strangers. She would be for him something he would add to the bric-a-brac on his mantelpiece, a porcelain princess to show his friends, and her own reality would be always diminished when she was with him. She knew now that despite the difficulties of our relationship I, at least, did not make her unreal to herself, and that the separation had been good because it had demonstrated to her where the only chance of her happiness lay, and we had both learned (the sky light now, the first pigeons cooing on the window ledge, an early truck backfiring in the empty dawn) how much we needed each other. I fell asleep with her in my arms, peacefully.

8

It was late October. On the Jersey shore, an hour from Atlantic City, there was a small summer place. It had once been a fishing village, and then a harbor for yachts. They still raced boats there, now and then, but at this time of the year the white dunes would be deserted. Would she like to go, now, this very minute?

She would love to go.

We could drive down and stay a day or so. There was nothing she needed to pack except a toothbrush and a nightgown, and she could put the nightgown into her little make-up case. It would be so nice to go away. The dunes were something we owed each other.

Yes, she said. We owed each other something like the dunes.

So in the afternoon we began to drive. The traffic was thin going through the tile of the Holland Tunnel with its contained roar, and Jersey beyond, once we were out on the highway, seemed an opener and a cleaner world. We headed down the coast. Having her with me, I was almost cheerful again, and there was a sense, to which I had become very unaccustomed, of a distinct sort of happiness. Having her with me transformed the landscape; and the trees, in their dying colors, and the stands which sold steamed clams, and the chicken farms, all pleased me: a small town seemed a nice place to be, and once more I regretted living so completely in New York.

I thought of the long white empty dunes and the wind blowing in from the ocean. We would stay in one of the small cottages or at a little hotel and take a long walk on the beach in the morning. She would like it. Autumn, she always said, was her weather. She was always happiest when the sky was clouded over and gray, and there was a fine delicate mist in the air. Summer with its heat and its unchanging sun depressed and exhausted her. She sat now, silently, in her fur coat, in a corner of the car, looking out at the view.

It's a nice view, I said.

Yes.

Know what?

She turned slightly.

What?

I love view, I said.

The little deserted settlement would be a lovely place to be reconciled. Everything that had happened would be forgotten once we were out on the dunes, walking and watching the gulls, and once we were warm together in a big hotel double bed. Perhaps there would be a fireplace in the room. A fireplace would be about perfect. I had promised myself not to mention anything that could possibly distress her to distress me and I meant very much to keep my mind turned away from everything that had happened. I would not ask, for asking would only endanger us again, what she had done or what her life had been in all the weeks we had been separated. There was nothing any more to be insisted upon, or described, for I was quite sure that what I had suffered had changed and purged me, and that somewhere a man, better than the man I had been, was finally emerging. There would be these two or three perfect days of wind and sand and love between us. Even now, the quick countryside, the odor of smoke in the bright air, the thin early moon, were beginning the change. I turned to her. Happy? I said.

It's wonderful to get away, she said.

From what?

Us. Them. It, she said.

We had been driving now about three hours. With the light failing, we turned inward toward the shore itself, and there, beyond a wooden bridge, and over the great flats of sand, and under a sky that was enormously empty, tiny beside the ocean, were the small white quiet houses that together made up the little settlement which I had remembered as being so beautiful and which I had always thought I would come back to some-day. The road was bad now, the great beach deserted, there was nobody at the post office and the little general store was closed, the white four-square church locked up, and the one hotel I remembered, not really a hotel but a place to stay at, was shut down too. I had not realized that nearly all the houses were just summer houses. Everything, even the church, closed when the summer was over and the people who owned the houses went away. It would all reopen in the spring. She was very disappointed. It was as beautiful as I had promised her it would be. We got out of the car and walked along the dunes. Oh, she said, why do they have to be closed? I imagined that, later, in the deep winter, great gales must strike at this lonely beach, and the tides become huge. We watched the gulls awhile, as the sky darkened, and then we returned to where I had parked the car. The sand sprayed under the wheels. We drove back over the narrow wooden bridge, and the boards rattled as the car went over them. It was colder now, with the sun gone; and I had forgotten gloves; and there was no heater in the car. There was nothing to do since we had come this far but go on; and there was no place to stay at but the tourist cabins and the drive-ins along the highway, and she did not want to stay at a cabin or a drive-in, and neither did I. It was begin-ning to go wrong; I could feel, in the car, as I drove, that she was disappointed, and tired, and cold; and the only place I could think of to spend the night was Atlantic City. I knew that it was bad to say Atlantic City to her: it was just the opposite of the kind of place we wanted to go; but it was dark now, and the countryside seemed barren of any life except the life of the beer taverns and the filling stations, and there was no place that I was sure of but Atlantic City. I thought that now she must be feeling that even when we planned a trip like this it went wrong, that it was hopeless to expect that anything we did together would ever go right. I thought if she had gone away with Howard he would have had all the conveniences arranged in advance. I thought that possibly she was thinking that too.

We'll only stay the night in Atlantic City, I said, and then in the morning we'll find someplace small.

She nodded. Atlantic City would be all right. But the look of pleasure had disappeared from her face.

My hands were freezing now on the wheel; and to warm it, I put my right hand under her fur coat on her thigh, and we drove like that, through the cold darkness. She fell asleep. It was ten o'clock when the highway broadened and the lights multiplied and there was Atlantic City, feeling all wrong as we came into it with its shabby dirty-sand look, but I was cold now, and hungry, and wanted a hot shower, and I woke her up. She looked blankly at the town; where are we? she said. She rubbed the sleep out of her eyes, and shivered. She stared at the boarding houses and the chain stores and the middle-aged people on the porches. It looks horrible, she said. I drove to one of the big hotels near the ocean, thinking that a big hotel would be at least something, and a doorman blew a whistle for the parking lot attendant while I went in and signed the hotel register. A bellhop took what small luggage we had up in the elevator. The lobby had been enormous, gilded, and deadly silent, and now the corridor, too, was enormously long, thickly carpeted and deadly silent. The season was over, except for the late conventions, leaving behind this somnolent hotel, like a huge animal that slept through the winter. The corridor was like that, dark and warm and sleeping and not quite alive. There were shrouded sofas and shrouded chairs they had moved out of suites they were redecorating, and the house telephone sitting on its small table under a gilded mirror looked about as lonesome as any instrument waiting to be used could possibly look. The silence, the not being used look everything had, the locked doors, door after door, all painted a hotel white and all with their one doorknob and their one keyhole and their one identifying number, made me feel as though she and I and maybe the bellhop were the only things alive in the hotel, and that if I listened carefully I would hear from these walls a deep subterranean snore. There were twin beds in the room. The bellhop opened the door of a closet which had an automatic light that went on when you opened the door. It was something the hotel seemed proud of. He pulled a window up and lowered a blind and snapped on two of the four or five table lamps and went out with a thank you sir after I tipped him. The room was comfortable enough, and warm, though, with the hotel steam hissing softly in the hotel radiator, and the hotel drapes, which were long and flowered and too vivid, like the pajamas a certain kind of girl would wear, billowed a little in the cold wind blowing in from the sea. She went to the window.

The sea. It was what we had come for, really. She pulled up a large chair, upholstered in roses, and sat there at the window with her fur coat still on and her face pressed to the pane looking out into the darkness loud with the sound of the surf. Below, on the late and now nearly deserted boardwalk, the lamps were hooded with mist. On the beach, shadowed now, there were stands of some kind, bleachers and a platform, arranged for what had been probably the Labor Day beauty contest and not yet dismantled, sad now with all the bunting gone from them, the judges, the girls in their bathing suits. Only the small motorized sedan chairs were left and I could see one or two chairs still being driven slowly along the boardwalk. Beyond was the water, nothing but water, dark under a dark sky, a sky with all its stars obscured, and fog blowing in across the sands. She sat there at the window, staring out at that darkness, as if looking long enough and being quiet enough would draw that wet, sad but not unpleasant silence and lightlessness into her, and spread it through her, until she shared it and was part of it, the far awayness of it, the being forever quietness of it. I turned off the table lamps the bellhop had snapped on, so that the darkness of the room moved out to meet the darkness of the sea moving in, and left her there at the window while I went into the bathroom to lay out my razor and toothbrush and to see if the water in the shower was hot. I took a shower, and when I came out of the bathroom she was still sitting there at the window and still looking out to where the water and the sky and the darkness all became one. I crossed to the window and kissed her.

Are you all right? I asked.

She was all right.

Then what was it?

It was nothing; it was just the ocean.

Because it's sad?

It wasn't sad, she said; no, that wasn't it. Sadness was the wrong word. It was just the ocean, and the darkness, the great darkness, how it went on and on. It was the being lost in it for a little while. You're tired, I said. There were at least fifteen taps in the bathtub, including one for salt water, and maybe one for taffy, but the water was hot. Why didn't she go and take a hot shower? A hot shower would be fine. She would feel wonderful after a hot shower.

She rose obediently. She took her coat off, finally, then stepped out of her skirt, and removed her sweater, and went toward the bathroom. I heard the door close. I went to the window and sat in the chair she had been sitting in. Looking out, as she had done, I tried to imagine what it was she had felt; the darkness did really after a while possess you, with the hypnotic crash of the surf, and there was a feeling almost of knowing, or being on the edge of knowing, what had been hidden from you, a deceptive simplification, and later, when I thought about it, I realized it was just a feeling, and that whatever it was that was on the verge of being understood disappeared as soon as you turned away from the window and faced again the room you were in, with the furniture someone else had put there, and the rather ugly hard somewhat obscene chaise longue occupying the middle of the floor. The shower was going strongly in the bathroom. I went to one of the twin beds and drew back the bedspread and lay down. The pillows had a starched fresh look, and the room now was just warm enough. I wondered what it would be like if finally we ever understood everything. I thought of the times I had experienced something like the feeling the dark ocean had given me, a feeling that came when one was just on the point of falling asleep, and how in the morning you had a feeling that the night before you had really and finally understood something. But evidently it was too difficult a thing for the mind to hold or keep, or perhaps it was too dangerous a thing for the mind to hold or keep, and we always fell asleep just where the knowledge we were about to acquire became dangerous to us. The door opened and she came out of the bathroom, glowing a little from all the hot water, and crossed the rug barefooted to the other twin bed and got quickly under the bedspread. I thought that the impact of the shower had steamed out of her all that dark feeling. She was shivering a little, trying to get warm under the spread, though it was not cold in the room. I waited a while, and then I got up from the other bed and crossed to hers. It would have been nicer to have had a double bed, and I should have thought of asking the night clerk; but in any other country they would have had double beds in rooms like these without having to ask. I did not see how the hotel people, whoever they were, could actually think there were customers who came to someplace like Atlantic City and asked for a room facing the ocean and then expected to find twin beds in it. It was all that goddamn pretending it wasn't so. Double beds, that was the first thing I was going to legislate for when I was President. Was I going to be President? Of course; and she was going to be, if she moved over, Congress.

I had forgotten in the weeks we had been separated how small she was, and I thought (the smallness made me think of it) how easily she could disappear again, how precarious my hold upon her was. She lay there, her back toward me, her face half buried in the clean laundered pillow, unresponsive. Everything depended, my sleeping peacefully, my being able to work, my confidence in myself, upon the only bond by which I held her, the words, extracted not always quickly from her, that she loved me. I had to assume that it existed, this invisible love which made itself visible not really too frequently in a gesture or a caress and showed itself not really too often in a softening of her voice or her eyes. But why, I said to myself, lying there, should I demand eternal proofs, eternal reassurance? She was not too demonstrative a girl; she said many times that it was difficult for her to show her feelings. Besides, this should be enough: that she was here, now, warm, with our legs interlaced, with my mouth against the skin, moist and smooth, of her back, with my hands touching all her moistness and smoothness. She was close, now, and actual enough, and surely this was a proof of a kind, a reassurance of a kind. If there was in me some fear of loss, some dread of abandonment, some anxiety which only reluctantly believed that I was loved, still there was something, also, which argued that she was not lying, that she did love me, that I had only to accept and to believe for the love to become real, so that doubt and belief, trust and distrust existed in me side by side, stretched out in me as we were stretched out together, their contradictory arms about each other.

She was so quiet, so still. She was far out there where the water ended and there was nothing but darkness. When I kissed her, or pressed against her, she did not respond. We had been driving six hours and there were all those weeks apart and now this. Outside, there was a long sough of wind; then the surf, growling; then a gull's high thin sound. Once again I was being excluded. I was alone in the twin bed, really; she was somewhere else, where I could not follow or reach her, somewhere the ocean I almost now disliked had taken her. She was enduring my mouth, enduring my hands. I touched her throat, thinking of the teethmarks which no longer disfigured it; first the teethmarks, then the long weeks, then this. I knew what she wanted: I was to lie there, as inert, as silent as she was, to caress her gently, to be there and not be there. I was to act out the game of her own melancholy with her. I turned her roughly toward me, forcing her legs open; her head moved sharply on the pillow as though she had been awakened, and she gave a short cry that was half caught in her throat and her fingers clawed for a moment as I lifted her toward me. I thought that wherever it was she had gone to, this would bring her back, and wherever it was she had locked herself up, this would open it, and wherever it was she was hidden, this would bring her forth. She would reappear, like an apparition, with the scream of final satisfaction. But except for the short cry she had uttered as I turned her, there was nothing; no scream, nothing; and except for her clawed fingers she did not resist and she did not struggle; there was nothing; there was acceptance, nothing. I fell away from her, defeated. She lay with her face half buried again in the pillow, lost, boneless; my taking her as I had, had widened the distance between us; she was still there, wherever the ocean had her, and locked up wherever she was locked up, and I hated her now. I suspected that now she regretted having taken the trip at all, and I was sick of the endless disappointments I seemed always to experience with her, the endless silences into which she plunged us. I would have to go on forever enduring the weight of her melancholias: oceans, gulls, a run in her stockings, a sad song, an item in the newspapers about a child dying somewhere of sleeping sickness, anything anywhere could cloud her over, and leave me again with a choked disappointment, a hope turned dull and irritable. She expected a great deal from me if what she expected was that I would forever be there to patiently witness her silences, and patiently accept the isolation of lying like this on a bed in which she had abandoned me. I was quite sure that on those gala nights she had gone with Howard to whatever club it was they had gone to or whatever home, she had managed miraculously to summon up a passably pleasant laugh, she had unearthed somehow a small sparkle to carry with her for the evening. She did not answer; she looked still as though she had fallen from a great height; her face remained averted. Was it because of the hotel? Or the bellhop, or registering, or how the curtains looked? Or the ugly chaise longue? I wasn't responsible for the interior decorating, nor had I designed the hotel, nor had I shrouded those dead chairs in the corridor. She had been cold in the car; asleep, hungry; there was nowhere else to drive this late at night. One ought at least to be discriminating about what one picked to be humiliated by. She said at last: I'm not humiliated. Then what in Christ's name was wrong? Nothing. That endless nothing; that persistent nothing; that nothing that always turned out to be the cause of everything. It was true I often sulked; that I was sometimes sullen; that now and then I was morose. I did not (I was sure) burden her with the dark consequences of my moods; the vultures worked privately on my liver. Besides, she had called; I was beginning to be all right again, I was getting so I could sleep. She had, with that famous accuracy of hers, picked exactly that more or less auspicious moment to telephone. Shouldn't I have? she said. Now it was I who did not answer. She said, at last: What is it you want from me? I lay there, in the darkness, wretched. She had looked into the mirror: O God, she had thought. She had screamed all right: perhaps she hadn't with me. But she had all right when he had bitten her. Tenderly, in his bathroom, a luxurious one, she had applied cold cream; the bruised skin was already turning an inevitable purple. I was to forget all this; easily, of course; it was something that did not even astonish her that she expected me to forget. How fortunate it was that he did not wear false teeth. Imagine, just like that, finding a loose pair of uppers randomly attached to you. I'd bet, though, she hadn't been distant then; nor melancholy; she reserved her melancholies for me; I had all the beauty of them. She managed, somehow, with him, to be fun, fun enough at least for him to bury his incisors a considerable depth in her. Then, having cold creamed that fleur de lis, she had returned to the bedroom, where on the pillow there were still traces of her warmth, and here and there, lost in the bed linen, a tiny curled black hair. That was the extraordinary indulgence I was to show, and that was the pleasant obscenity I was to forget. And you can't, can you? she said. Something should have warned me; but it had become impossible for me to stop the machinery of my own venom. I heard her say in a voice that had flattened itself and was colder than any voice she had ever used with me before: What do you want from me?

Nothing.

Not a goddamn thing, now.

She got up and walked to the big ugly flowered chair on which her clothes lay disarranged. She began to get dressed. It was not what I had expected. I had expected tears, I had expected her to be unbearably goaded, I had expected her to confess some consciousness of her own guilt. But there were no tears; no reproaches. She had, at last, found the intricate comedy of our reconciliations intolerable. Some fatigue had hardened in her, and she was determined now not to endure any more those terrible cross-examinations to which I subjected her nor those theatrical torments in which I would be caught. I watched her, stupefied, draw on her sweater, snap the waistband of her skirt tight; I watched her step into her shoes. It was hopeless. I would punish her endlessly for that night. I would torment her forever. The forgiveness had been, after all, another ruse, another falsehood. I hated her, now, absurdly, for taking my suffering too seriously. I would have required only that she endure it for a while. Her punishment should have been in the enduring of it. But she was past enduring, or so she thought. She was finished with something, and she wanted nothing now but to be out of this overelaborate and over-flowered bedroom, and home again on her own couch, alone. I got up, stiffly, and dressed. We did not speak to each other. When I was dressed I went into the bathroom and packed again the few toilet articles I had only so short a time before unpacked. I left the closet door open so that the automatic light would, I hoped, burn itself out or at least increase the hotel's electric bill, and we went down the corridor, and waited for the elevator. We were again enemies. It was almost one o'clock in the morning. I checked out at the desk and the night clerk, see-ing we had registered only three hours ago, asked if there was something wrong with the room; and I said no, the room was fine, we were on our way to Florida and liked driving at night, while the boy took our bags and put them in the back of the car. It was very cold now. Outside, I looked toward the beach; a tired pennant still flew from the top of some pole erected on the sand. Dark, huge, the ocean swept out toward Europe. Ten miles out of Atlantic City we said the only words to each other we said the whole drive home.

I'll tell you what's wrong.

She said: What?

I said: Us. Them. It.

9

I've always thought there is nothing quite like the sight of a man at eight o'clock in the morning, dressed in a business suit, and with his face shaved and his tie knotted and a briefcase under his arm, having a quick coffee at an orange stand where already the frankfurters are glossily turning on a hot griddle. I've always thought there is no face quite like the face of a young girl, with her lipstick on and the exact pencilings of her eyebrows, coming up out of the subway and trying to make it to the office on time. I've always thought there is nothing sadder anyplace than seeing what people look like early in the morning as they go to work. I wasn't going to work. I was driving home from a trip to Jersey a girl with whom I had had what I was sure was my final bitterness and my last quarrel, and she was sitting, small and tight and huddled up, in a corner of the car, waiting for an unendurable ride to be over. It was over at last, with my halting the car outside the door of the house she lived in, and she gathered her things up, her purse and the small make-up case in which she had so carefully folded a nightgown, while a man in a cap at a news-stand on the corner was crying the morning editions and in a department store you could see the salesgirls fixing the counters at which they worked, and she got out of the car, slamming the car door. She did not say good-by; still furious, if what she was was furious, she disappeared into the vestibule. I thought to myself:

this is how you last saw her; disappearing, dirty, exhausted, angry, carrying a small make-up case, a street door swinging closed, and I didn't think I cared. I put the car in gear, and went home, and fell asleep immediately, and slept thickly until late afternoon.

That was the morning I had the odd dream: I was in a sort of clearing, in a wood, and there was a semicircle of girls in white gowns, somewhat Greek, seated on the grass, watching somebody in the multi-colored costume of an acrobat performing astonishing leaps in the air. The girls were very pleased with the performance as the acrobat succeeded in going higher and higher, twirling his ankles, with each leap. He had just performed a really stupendous one, possibly the greatest leap of his career, high above the lifted heads of the seated girls in white, when there was a sound like the air hissing out of a punctured tire, a distinct fizzing sound, and down he came to crumple on the grass. I could see him lying there, on the grass, and one of the girls came over to the acrobat, and touched him with the tip of a naked foot. She said: It's empty. And it was. There was nothing but a costume there on the ground. I woke up thinking of her disappearing into the vestibule, and it seemed to me that I, too, no longer cared how it ended, gracefully or ugly, that I had come to the end of all the possible feelings about her I could ever have. I ate breakfast, and then I thought vaguely of calling someone or going to see someone but there was no one I really wanted to talk to or see, and I went instead for a walk along the East River. I was determined not to call her, because while it was true that I had promised myself not to say anything to her on the trip and then I had said it in Atlantic City, still it was understandable, and the least she could have done in that hotel room was have realized that what I was doing was understandable. The drive along the river was still being paved, as it seemed always being paved, and the

earth was everywhere excavated, and at the time they were
still working on the skeleton of the United Nations building
with a determination, apparently, to make it the really out-
standing architectural horror of the day. I remember thinking
that what they were evidently trying to do with it was get it
real flat and when they had it flat enough why they would just
slip the statesmen in sideways. That didn't seem to me too bad
an idea. In Tudor City there were the usual starched children
playing with the usual dogs and watched by the usual nurses: I
thought the number of Irish and English nurses had diminished, and there were more colored ones. That, too, might be,
like the UN building, a sign of progress. I was beginning to
feel almost invulnerable again, but it was a deceptive feeling,
for I had neglected to notice that my anger had vanished, and
as it vanished I was beginning to not exactly regret the abrupt
termination of what would have been two really fine days, but
to put a more charitable interpretation upon her fury with me,
and her coldness. After all, I had tormented her. After all, it was
an episode fixed in the past, and nothing, guilt or penitence,
could change it; what I had done, really, was to destroy the
possibilities of my own pleasure. We would have left Atlantic
City in the morning, and the obscure melancholy would have
gone with that grotesque hotel, and further down the coast
we would have found some small place where she would have
been cheerful and happy. But I had spoiled it all. There were
twinges of something like remorse; a flash of something like
shame. For a brief instant it seemed to me that I detected in
myself something which had wanted deliberately to ruin the
possibility of the trip's being a happy one; that I had wanted it
to end as it did, so badly; that it had not been unpremeditated.
But it went away, quickly. Evening was falling now; the first
lights came on, mild and autumnal; there were odors from the
tenements of all the dinners being somewhere invisibly cooked,

the sound of pots being somewhere rattled, and of women's voices. Something like a sigh was being exhaled from the city; I thought of my mother, with her corset loosened. Perhaps I should, since she must be miserably unhappy now, and I, even if I had not entirely caused the unpleasantness between us, was at least partly responsible for it, perhaps I should be the one to make the conciliatory gesture now; she had, after all, made hers when she had telephoned me. It was impossible to expect any girl, her particularly, since she had her pride, to feel, because of a miscalculation, eternally humble; did I expect her to spend the remainder of her life on her knees? And was it really so unendurable, the thought of those teethmarks? Hadn't I exaggerated their obscenity? She had tried to make amends as best she could; why should I insist upon amends she could not possibly make? I found myself thinking that among the things wrong with me was living at a hotel, and that it was the hotel that had somehow subtly caused the appalling way I had behaved. I told myself that someday soon I would move, perhaps to the West Side, near the Hudson. I ought to live somewhere permanently: a small room, high up, very simple, facing the river, with, late at night, long walks up the Drive. I had convinced myself that a life, severely simple, made up of hard work and solitude, was the life I really wanted, and I was experiencing in advance some of the healing effects of living near the river in that magically bare room, and I had thought that in an hour or so I would telephone and ask, not for forgiveness but for a truce of a kind, when, having walked over to Fifth Avenue, I turned toward Rockefeller Plaza. There were crowds heavily leaning over the stone rampart looking down at the skaters in the skating rink. There was a rather stout man, in a checkered cap, clowning on the ice, and a little girl, completely costumed, doing astonishing figure eights and leaps, and a couple, she in a mink coat, he in a tuxedo, arm in arm, who must have thought it would be fun skating before dinner. I went down through the people watching into the English Grill to have a drink, and there was Vivian, in a short black velvet skating skirt, having a hot toddy at the bar. Lover, she said, how nice to see you. The hot toddy, steaming in its thick glass, looking medicinal as hell, was wonderful on a cold night, and she really went skating because half the fun was sitting at the bar in the short flaring costume, ordering a toddy; besides, she loved the trouble it put the bartender to.

She examined me.

How nice and fat I looked. What had happened to the rumored torch? She'd heard it was blazing. I didn't look at all, not to her aged eyes, as though I were carrying anything so combustible as a torch. I looked rather disgustingly benign. Was I sure I didn't want a hot toddy, now that I looked so disgustingly benign?

No.

She drank the smoking toddy.

So the torch was out. How nice. She wished hers would blow out too, thoroughly. But it was nice somebody's had. I ought to go skating, now that I seemed about to resume the dimensions of an ordinary and torchless human being; skating was wonderful, too, in a way, the exercise, so much nicer than all that sticky business of suffering, she recommended it, skating, and a steak, and dinner together, since here she was and here I was, a pair of survivors. And yes, she'd almost forgotten, she'd seen my ex-girlfriend's ex-boyfriend. Last night, at the club.

Howard?

Yes, Howard. Looking perfectly miserable, too. She'd left him, I knew that, didn't I?

Yes, I knew that.

She'd probably call me any day now, and I could, benign

94

though I was, pick right up where I'd left off. Of course, she was rather marvelous, when you thought about it, asking him pointblank like that if he was going to marry her. What could the poor son of a bitch say but no?

Did I say something? Vivian said. My God, she called you. You didn't know.

God, women, Vivian said. I wondered why you seemed so well. And with that angelic look, too. What in hell does that mother of hers feed her to give her such an angelic look?

Now, lover, Vivian said. If I knew you were going to look like that, I'd have kept my big mouth shut.

She really didn't tell you? she said. She's wonderful. You'd think she couldn't stick a pin in a pincushion. She just called you in the middle of the night. She discovered she didn't love him. I'd never have thought of a simple explanation like that. Which is my trouble: I'm always thinking of the complicated ones, and they never work. Will you do me a favor and stop looking so devastated? Any minute I'll start feeling I just strangled a baby in the crib.

Where are you going? she said.

I left her at the bar.

Was she home? Vivian said. Well it's only five-thirty. Relax. She really didn't two-time you: she just got her signals crossed a little. Why don't you drink that Scotch before it dies in the glass?

And the way he cried on my shoulder, Vivian said. I'd have felt sorry for him if there hadn't been such a cover charge. She's gotten under that skin of his, too, and I suppose, with all his money, he never thought she would just stand up and walk. Now he thinks because she went he's lost a fine girl. Does it sound familiar? Darling, everything's familiar. He was certainly groaning. I must say there's nothing duller than listening for two hours on end to somebody else's love troubles. And he

was so stiff about it. He's probably been out all afternoon trying to get rid of it on the handball court. I got the impression
though that his resistance wasn't going to last very long: he
looked about ripe for the telephone routine.

And meanwhile she called you.

Marvelous, Vivian said. Some women are, you know: they
don't walk erect yet, but in a way they're marvelous.

What do you want his address for? she said. In the first place
I don't know it, and in the second place you're not going to do
something immensely heroic, are you, like breaking in on
them if she's with him? You don't know if she's with him: she
may just be out, somewhere, looking at trousseaus.

Can't you see her though, Vivian said, the night she asked
him? She probably sat perfectly upright, the little soldier, and
looked him straight in his dividends. I suppose she decided
she had given him long enough. I wonder what she wore for
the occasion? Something black? I imagine she felt as though
her virginity was being miraculously restored. I suppose if he
could have gotten away with anything but a direct no, which
she forced from him, he would have. Then she went home, and
took an aspirin, and cold-creamed her face, and since she wasn't
going to lose everything she called you. I am being bitchy,
aren't I? Well, like my doctor says, rich or poor, money makes
a difference.

Do you know she fainted once in an unemployment insur-
ance office? Vivian said. Keeled right over.

And then there's the kid, she said. Lovely little girl. What is
she now, five? She played some records once she had made:
mama whispering the lyrics, and baby singing, in a sweet
falsetto, something out of *Annie Get Your Gun*. Darling little
girl; and smart. She'd marry Dracula, I suppose, to protect the
kid. So don't be stupid: she can't help herself. Of course, she
could be honest about it, but it's late in the day, and I wouldn't

say this is exactly the century to start being honest in. She has to persuade herself that he has other virtues besides that monstrous bank account. Besides, a cold bitch couldn't have gotten him, if she gets him. It needed that small childish affrighted smile of hers. That tremulousness. That little delicate chin quivering when she's on the point of tears. That look, when she's hurt, as though someone just swatted her with a heavy rose.

Sit still, Vivian said. Drink your Scotch. Being nervous isn't going to change anything.

Yes, I've seen them together, she said: he pilots her a little, by the elbow, as though she'll run aground somewhere if he isn't careful. That wife of his, the first cutie, she must have really gone over him with a rough brush. Afterward, what he couldn't get was: who'd love him? Really him. Which one meant it, the babe with the trusting eyes, the demure sweetie who cooed at him and wouldn't let him touch even the edges of a half-exposed breast in an evening gown, and which one was taking him for a well-known sleighride? He couldn't ever be sure. Because there was nothing in the world to separate for him in advance the good ones from the bad ones: they all looked alike in clothes from Saks. So he's gun-shy, and the one, strangely enough, he trusts least is himself. He knows the error is always finally his. Now, I suppose, he's in love with her, and convinced, too, because she's gone, that she's what she pretends she is: the piano student, the nice little girl who commutes home. But it's all tentative with him: he'll have detectives out watching her get out of her bubble bath if he ever gets the slightest suspicion she's not quite made of snow apples and pure-brand foods.

God knows what they talk to each other about, Vivian said. She's not the most brilliant conversationalist in town, and while he doesn't grunt, I wouldn't like an extended tête-à-tête for the next twenty years with him. It's that damned idea of his that what he's saying is automatically interesting because he's saying it. And he's never anything but earnest. Do you suppose having more than sixty-five dollars in the bank all at one time would make that kind of a square out of me? Because, brother, if there's a dull opinion left in the world, he has it. I mean he'd drive me out of what mind I have. He'll tell you, for example, about some mine he's just, more or less as a joke, put a few thousand in, fifty or sixty he means, expecting the people out there at the mine, he's never even seen the goddamn thing, to bring in only a little lead or a little silver, and somebody took a wrong turn, amnesia no doubt, and opened up an accidental vein of solid gold. They're bringing the stuff in in carloads. And of course he says it all modestly, with a cute little deprecatory smile, amused by it all: the son of a bitch, amused by a vein of solid gold. That's what I mean. That would drive me out of my head. And then the friendships he boasts about, and drops neatly into the conversation: Sam, because of his horses, Sam being some San Francisco millionaire, and the horses being a racing stable; or Jack, who's taking him big game hunting one of these days in Kenya, a two-gun safari, and you're supposed to know what a two-gun safari is; or Ed, the newspaperman, the newspaper being, it turns out, a chain of them, who's a real good egg but lacks perspective; then it turns out what he means by perspective is that Ed, the thoughtless fellow, gets into political quarrels, antagonizing all sorts of people he might need later, like Senators. I'd go crazy trying to talk to a man who does that with the English language. And then that laugh of his: I mean at what he thinks are jokes, little cracks about sex: they really kill him. And then, the rich conservative businessman's horror of publicity. Mustn't get his name in the papers, the gossip columns particularly; but he loves it. The poor bastard is really dying to be glamorous, after all. They're all dying to be glamorous. That's what they're doing in those clubs. Now where are you going? Vivian said.

The phone rang emptily in the room she wasn't in.

Darling, relax, Vivian said. She'll be home. She has to come home sometime just like I have to go home sometime. We all have to go home sometime. Where else is there?

Now let's get on the sex thing, Vivian said. That would really knock me out. And let me explain why. Well in the first place he would be just the kind of a gent who would figure it all out in that solid little skull of his that it was all right with a tootsie he picked up in the lobby of a hotel in Miami Beach or on a trip to Nassau but not with his little wife. There are certain well-known practices that one doesn't ever practice with one's little wife in the sanctity of one's little home. Of course the little wife, meek and mild and heaven's child, might have more or less of a yen for a practice like that or any other kind of infield practice but something, what the hell would you call it, honorableness I guess he thinks it is, says to him it ain't the sort of scrimmage one indulges in with the lady of the house. Because if you do and she likes it then how the hell, once more, do you tell the difference between her and the twenty-dollar thing you picked up in the lobby in Miami Beach? And brother, like I said, he wants to be able to tell the difference. But she's going to marry him. He could have two heads and she'd marry him, but I suppose my telling you all this won't make the slightest bit of difference to you. No matter how much information of the most revealing kind you stick in a man's head what he's going to do he'll do anyway, like leave a perfectly nice bar with a perfectly nice glass of Scotch and canned music and all, and go out and try to kick in somebody's perfectly inoffensive door. Why? That's a good question, isn't it, lover, and I'll bet you haven't the slightest inclination to answer it. Well, goodnight. Save a stained-glass window for me.

Outside, I caught a taxi.

She came out of the house, pulling on long black gloves, wearing over her hair a light gray filmy scarf, and as she turned toward the corner a drunk came lurching out of the bar and grill, and I watched her swerve slightly to avoid him. She was all dressed up. She gave the drunk a look that was meant to wither him but which, unfortunately, the drunk did not notice, and from the other side of the street I watched her turn down the avenue. She was apparently walking to wherever she was going. I was sure I knew where she was going. It was about seven o'clock, the hour when they let the beasts into the adjoining cages. At the corner a red light delayed her. She adjusted something on her wrist: a bracelet, or her watch. Somebody in a homburg standing outside a drugstore looked at her as she went by: the filmy scarf first, and then her legs. A taxi slowed thinking she was a fare.

O you bitch, I thought.

She hesitated briefly outside a dress shop on Park: a dummy in the window wore a dress that was brighter than the lipstick on her mouth. She looked critically at the gown, sparing it, I thought, a precious moment or two, but evidently something about it displeased her. Was it cut too low? Or perhaps not low enough. I was sure the gown wasn't cut low enough. She liked a good subterranean cut in her evening gowns, they went so nicely with her demure expression. She walked on, looking like any girl would look around dinnertime hurrying to a date, with a touch of perfume behind each ear, a touch of perfume between her upstanding little breasts, and, providing the date was special enough and consequential enough, just the merest touch between her legs.

Bitch, bitch, I thought.

Hurry, hurry, she had said, and I had hurried, in the dead of night, to her palpitating side. Now, mounted on her little motorcycle, all dressed up, she was hurrying to what she must have known would inevitably happen all the time we were driving down to the little place on the shore, and have known all the time we were at the hotel, and she had only been making sure that I did not slip entirely away while she waited. She turned once, and I started guiltily, thinking she had seen me, moving back into the doorway of a camera store.

Bitch, bitch, bitch, I thought.

And now you're Hawkshaw, the cockeyed detective, I said to myself. Now you're the trained gumshoe, hot on her trail. Why don't you open a goddamn agency?

Subject (aged twenty-four, wearing a gray scarf, high-heeled shoes, a fur coat somewhat gone to hell, and a bitch if there ever was one) disappears momentarily between two parked cars, emerges again, a radiant babe, on her way to a roll in the hay. Or didn't they put that in the neat, typed-up, circumspect, but precise reports filed at the bureau, and mailed, with the customary discretion, to Mr X, the gentleman dying to know the truth? And what exactly was the truth I was dying to know? I knew it already, with a dead certainty, didn't I? I knew it, I knew everything now, I knew the customary everything. Then why was I following her, boy Pinkerton with my nickel badge, to a destination I was so absolutely sure I knew? Did old indomitable me still somewhere incredibly believe that she might not even now be going to where beyond the shadow of any doubt I knew she was going? There she was, the little intent wayfarer on life's difficult highway, with the slight dabs of perfume in their discreet places, while I, patsy on a monumental scale, followed half a block behind her. She'd smell real sweet tonight. She'd be a goddamn bouquet. She'd be lilies of the valley, with the dew still on them.

O you prize horse's ass!

Would Howard, too, overwhelmed by the first sight of her,

kneel? I thought not. I was more the kneeling type. I had a real talent for little exhibitions like that. Just show me a floor and down I went. He, the poor bastard, stayed upright and suffered. His money held him up, like a corset. He diminished her reality, did he? He treated her like bric-a-brac? He was the perfect stranger? I'd diminish her reality, I'd perfect stranger her now. She had no idea how I'd bric-a-brac her.

And so I watched her, moving determinedly ahead of me, intent upon herself, and I could almost see into that busy little brain as it prepared itself for the evening's adventures, and I could almost hear the fragmentary decisions she was so actively making, the little scenes she was playing out inside her mind. And I thought, suddenly, that all these women, accompanied or unaccompanied, alone or on the arms of men, going somewhere now on the street, must be enacting within themselves little dramas of copulation as equally calculated as hers. That, really, the city was nothing but a huge bedroom, with some office buildings attached, as they said in the army, for rations, and that for each of these women there was an absolute conviction that the universe was arranged for only one end: her in bed. That even to the withered dug of this old bat who passed me now, in furs, with her thin greedy still painted mouth, some man still clung and whimpered mama. She had turned a corner now, and I watched her as, with a nod to the doorman, she disappeared into a large imposing apartment hotel, and I was alone on the street, staring at a dog urinating against a fire hydrant, a boy on a bicycle, the banked windows any one of which in the nineteen stories could be his, my mouth twisted in a smile that tried to pretend what had happened was only what I had expected to happen. I thought a little wildly of storming past the switchboard; of breaking in on them. Disguised as what, a Fuller Brush man? The doorman shooed the investigative dog away; again, I hesitated. The agitation mounted in me. I was actually trembling; that coldly ill disastrous feeling had begun again in that vulnerable stomach of mine, and again some part of me had detached itself, and floated now, a short distance away, observing sardonically the picture I made standing there near a French hand laundry trying to X-ray those windows behind one of which she was now. Again, the sense mounted in me of having become something I was not, of having some creature emerge who inhabited me but was not me and who appeared only when I suffered. I could feel all sorts of idiotic plans and counterplots forming themselves in my mind: a childish confrontation of the doorman; an idea of purchasing flowers, and pretending I was to deliver them; entering the house boldly and announcing, in a self-assured voice, that I had an appointment: would they ring Mr X? Then I suddenly realized that I had apparently arrived in a position I had prepared for myself; for there had not been any need for me to be here now, on the street, pretending that I was an idle pedestrian, lurking in the shadow of the hand laundry, and that I could have intercepted her on the avenue if what I had really wanted was to intercept her and to prevent her from making the visit she was making or keeping the obscene appointment she was keeping. How simple it would have been to have stopped her on the street! And yet I hadn't; more, it had not even occurred to me. Again there was that inexplicable thing about my behavior! I had allowed her to go; I had, possibly, even wanted to have her go; and briefly again, it seemed to me, that in some horribly involved way it was I who was responsible for her being now where she was, in that house with him, and that I had wanted it, and had arranged it subtly so that she should be there. I walked abruptly away, and caught a taxi, and went back to my hotel. I knew now what I was going to do, and with it was the knowledge that in a way I had always known this would be what I would do, and that the denouement was not at all an accidental thing, something that chance had arranged, but that it was something which I had always known from the very first time she had told me about Howard and about the evening she had met him in the Club Paris. I went through the telephone directory until I found the house number of that imposing residence she had entered and then I telephoned. The house switchboard connected me, and I could hear, probably on its stand in the foyer, if there was a foyer, his phone ringing, and then somebody, I supposed it was the maid, answered, and when I asked for her there was a hesitant pause as though the maid wasn't sure that she ought to summon or interrupt them wherever they were, then evidently she decided it was after all none of her business and she called her to the phone. She came to the phone and when she said hello I knew that she knew intuitively that the voice would be mine, that I had managed somehow to reach her, and I could hear the anxious and placating note in her own voice. She was so thoroughly caught. I realized then that it was what I wanted: to have her pinned like that, and wriggling, on a hook. To have her where she could not any more escape. I told her exactly what I intended to do, the letter I intended to write, the details I intended to make clear; the choice was hers. She could stay there and have a lovely evening, and the letter would be delivered in the morning, or she could be at my hotel in twenty minutes. What, of course, I wanted, was to tear her away and if it was in the middle of an interrupted kiss all the better. It was all like something in a bad movie, if they still did things like that even in the movies; but mostly it was like something in a bad life. I hung up, and sat down to wait for her. I was quite confident that she could invent a sick grandmother or a cousin from out of town to explain the call. And confident, too, that with a little ingenuity she could convince him that she had left his number with her phone service, and that the call was one

she expected. In the half hour I waited for her to arrive, [k]now-
ing that she would arrive, and knowing I would despise h[er] [if]
she did and despise myself even more for having made her, [come,]
there were moments when my illness became so acute a wave
of dizziness passed over me, when I thought that it was impossible to endure any more. I put my head down upon the table as
though even to hold myself erect had become too much. I
wanted to crouch down somewhere in the darkness, to make
myself into a fetal ball. And always the other thing, that
detached eye, watched me, and was unalarmed. That levitated
sense of myself was not touched, and did not suffer; it sat up
there, on a stalk, as though nothing of any real consequence
was happening, as though I, writhing, was nevertheless sham-
ming, as though it neither believed nor disbelieved in my pain.
When I thought that perhaps I had been wrong, and that she
was not, after all, coming, she knocked on the hotel door.

She was being very thin-mouthed when she came in the door. My confidence in her ability to find an effective excuse had not been misplaced. She had invented a Fred from Los Angeles, a favorite cousin. She was somewhat frightened, too, I could see, because once again she imagined I was about to strike her, or might later strike her, and while she seemed willing to risk that, because it was after all only the normal sort of chance a woman took in so dangerous an enterprise as love, and even accepted the possibility, I could also see that she did not really believe that I intended to do what I had so carefully threatened to do over the phone. She had, in the taxi probably, convinced herself that I was incapable of anything so low as what I had threatened her with. She released now, like an injured bird, a smile that took off from her mouth, fluttered badly in the air, and sank unnoticed somewhere on the rug. A pot of coffee was percolating slowly on my small electric range. She gave up smiling – for Lent, I thought.

How did you find me? she said. Indignation seemed the more immediate tactic. Do you have detectives following me? Can't I do anything or go anywhere without having you trail after me, or telephone me, or come banging on a door?

(Banging on doors terrified her. There was something so public about it. She'd settle, I could see, for a black eye. Of the two, the black eye seemed the lesser consequence.)

She hesitated. I hadn't, after all, banged on the door.

Would you have, she said, if I hadn't come here? Would you have – she searched for the word as she did for the misplaced keys in her handbag – demeaned yourself that much? Demeaned surprised me; I hadn't anticipated demeaned. That she had found an appropriate word, however, seemed to renew her confidence and her indignation, which had faltered for a moment.

I suppose, she said, I'll never have a life of my own again simply because I was in love with you once. Isn't it permitted to end an affair with you? Do I have to be hounded and threatened and persecuted the rest of my life for it?

I thought she ought to sit down. She could be just as indignant seated. She refused a chair; she rejected the sofa. She had no intentions of staying. She was honoring me with a flying, and final, interview.

Her gloves annoyed her; as long as she had them on, she had an air of being about to decisively go. She removed one glove.

That was very stupid, she said, the things you said to me over the phone.

Were they?

She searched my face. Somewhere, I must not be entirely serious. I could hardly have meant those shameful alternatives: either she went to bed with me now, which of course she would rather die than do, or I would mail that letter, which of course was just as unthinkable.

She waited.

You can't be that low, she said. Somewhere, in that forbidding face of mine, there must have been still some trace of the me she knew and had loved. I could not possibly want now to spoil everything that had ever existed between us, and leave her with a memory of an evening as base as this. I must have somewhere the remnants of a sense of honor. I had been kind in the past, I had been thoughtful, I had cared for her. This wasn't me. She knew me better than that; she was so sure she knew me better than that. She walked across the room, nervously, glancing blindly at the coffee percolating on the electric range, as though it were an object she could not immediately identify. She searched the dustier corners of the room as though she were looking for an advocate to plead her cause. She was beginning to have difficulty believing I would not send the letter. What was it, she asked, that she had done that was so terrible and for which I was exacting this penalty? She had gone to his house. Hadn't I behaved abominably at the hotel? Hadn't we driven for five terrible hours together in the car without speaking to each other? It was impossible between us: the trip to Atlantic City had convinced her forever that it was impossible between us. Surely, I knew that too? But she was neglecting something; couldn't she, with the slightest of efforts, recall it? That wounded look, that persecuted air, that hysteria of innocence, contrived somehow to ignore what Vivian, sitting at the bar with a hot toddy, had told me, that the evening she had telephoned and I had come ignorantly to her side, it had been because he had not wanted to marry her, and I was, how should I put it: a patsy, a choice of desperation, second best, something rescued from the junk pile? How would she like it phrased? I had swallowed my own required number of toads, and I had found them not exactly the choicest item on the menu, and what I was doing was simply passing the taste for toads on to him. He loved her: he wanted her: he could afford swallowing a toad or two, as I had.

She looked at me: You think I'm a whore, don't you?

Think? I was sure.

She sat down on the sofa, now, and began to cry. Don't you touch me, she said: don't you come near me. There were admirable little choking effects between the tears. She couldn't, of course, find her handkerchief, and mine, which she refused, had ink on it. Seeing the ink she assumed I had already composed the letter. She appeared crushed.

In the smallest of voices she said: It's what I deserve for having fallen in love with you.

She blotted the tears with her glove.

I could send the letter now if that was what I wished. I could send it if that was the satisfaction I wanted. I had always doubted her. I had always thought as all men did that the woman they loved was a whore. Behind all my protestations had been that thought always: that she would cheat, that she wasn't to be trusted, that she was a whore. I could think what I liked now. It no longer mattered. I was being horrible. I enjoyed being horrible. It gave me some pleasure she would not even try to understand to be as horrible as I was being. She wished now only to forget I ever existed. She wished now only never to fall in love again. She swore she never would. She would enter a convent, she would stuff it up, but please God no more men. Never, never. It was horrible of me to give her that choice. To even dare think that she would allow me to blackmail her into going to bed with me. I was doing it only out of hate. Out of some horrible desire for revenge. It was no revenge. It would only humiliate us both. What pleasure could I possibly find in forcing her to undress the way a whore would undress and to get into a cold and unwanted bed? Why did I wish to wound myself so? Why did I want to dirty her and to dirty myself?

She should allow me then to send the letter, I said, and spare both of us that experience. He would forgive her. If he loved her he would forgive her as I had in the past. Or did she believe that forgiving her was a talent only I possessed?

But she was afraid to have me send the letter. I had no idea really what I would say in it. I could hardly have said much. And she could have always denied it. She had, I supposed, considered quickly how effective a denial would be. She had not very much faith evidently in its effectiveness. He would be suspicious even if she succeeded in making him believe that the letter was malicious and untrue. She had very little confidence in his forgiving her. It was something I contemptuously knew. It was that stiffness of his and that conviction of how right he was about his world. It was that night in the George Cinq and his unsureness about the women he chose. She could see however that there was something ridiculous in the whole idea of my writing a letter or even of a letter being written and mailed to him. It was dangerous but it was also ridiculous. The fact that I had thought of something as an instrument of revenge which was at once ridiculous, shameful and dangerous must have given her the hope that there was some way out of her dilemma. She felt that I could be prevented from doing anything at all if she could only summon up from some secret recess the words or the gestures or the expressions which would allow both of us to escape from a trap I had set for both of us. She seemed aware that it was not something quite real which was being played out between us but some necessary unreality which had to be dealt with as though it were real.

Besides, I said, I asked very little of her. She had only to go into the bedroom and prove to me conclusively how much she wanted him and how much she was prepared to do in order to have him. I wanted it as a simple demonstration that I had not been wrong about her. She could consider it if she wished as a morbid need on my part for demonstrable evidence. I wanted the pleasure of knowing something to be finally true. She ought not to feel quite so bad about it as she did: I was not, after all, a stranger, and I was not, after all, offering her the indignity of a thousand dollars. It was a transaction of a different kind, involving the education of an idiot. I was, of course, that idiot.

She no longer was quite ready to die rather than do it.

She said: Hit me if you want to. Or tear my clothes. Or anything. But you mustn't make me do this.

She looked inexpressibly weary. She showed only the color of her lipstick. She now saw that it was useless to talk to me. She would refuse to do what I so insanely wanted her to do not for her own sake but for mine. She had nothing now to look forward to. She had always been unlucky with men. She supposed it was her fate. I wished to destroy her. Very well, she would be destroyed. That too she would accept as her destiny, to be destroyed by someone she had loved. It was true that the night she had telephoned she had been frightened. She deserved what had happened because she had trusted Vivian. She had thought Vivian her friend. She knew now nobody was her friend and nobody truly loved her. Vivian had been envious of her good fortune and I was horrible. She had a right to be frightened. She was alone. She had thought I loved her. She knew now I didn't. I never had. She was only a girl and she had a right to be frightened.

You don't believe me, she said. You think I'm lying.

It was because she had wanted so much to be happy. Why was that so difficult for me to understand? She was a girl. She was defenseless. She wanted to be happy. I might laugh if I wished at something so stupid. Stupid she might be. She felt worthless enough as it was. She knew now she had no talent. That she was useless. That she could neither play well enough nor sing well enough nor do anything well enough. And it was not for her own sake she was doing what she had to do. It was for Barbara's sake. She had been so frightened when her father left. She had not let her leave her bedside for a long time at night. She had had to stay with her and promise her that she would not ever go away or leave her with anybody until the child fell asleep. She had been a failure as a wife and a failure as a singer. The least she could do was try not to be a failure as a mother. She had felt so terrible during the divorce. I had no idea what it meant to feel that one was responsible for depriving a child of its father. Was that what she was guilty of, not wanting to be that kind of a failure too? Was she a whore, was she bad, was she dishonest? She no longer knew. She knew only that everything had ended.

We could go to bed now if that was what I wished. I would feel worse about it than she would. The degradation would be mine. The humiliation would be really mine. I had succeeded in dragging us both down together. Going to bed really made no difference any more. She would do it because she could see I was suffering so. Because it was a revenge I so mistakenly thought I needed. She would be cold. She would be colder than ice. But if that was what would help me because she wanted to help me she would do it knowing of course that it was insane and would not help.

The great mistake, she said, had been our ever falling in love. We had never been meant for each other. But that was not why now she was leaving me. I knew quite well why she was leaving me. I had always known.

Nobody was necessary to me, she said. Not really necessary. I was fond enough of people and some I loved but none of them were necessary to me. She had never been necessary to me. She wanted to be somebody's sun and moon and stars. She wanted them to die without her. She wanted them to need her always and forever. That was stupid, too. I would think that was stupid, too. There was nothing she could ever really do for me but go to bed. It was the least of the things a woman wanted to do for a man. I would get tired of that and when I was tired there would be nothing else that she had to give me. I existed for myself. She did not mean that I was selfish. I existed for myself. That was what frightened her. It was what always frightened a woman. She was not a monster or bad or even calculating.

I had made her out bad and calculating and a monster because she had slept with me and then with him and then ran back to me and then ran back to him. I had always insisted it was the money. It was partly the money. Yes, why should she pretend the money had nothing to do with it? But the funny thing was with all the money he still needed her in a way I never would and what he felt for her was something I would never feel for a woman. She meant something to him. She had lied about her being only a piece of bric-a-brac because she thought it was something I would think was true of them. But it had not been true: he needed her, she had an importance. A woman was not really important to me except perhaps when I was a little sick or a little lonely or a little frightened. She used to think it was because I was somewhat like her first husband: that she couldn't touch me. But it wasn't that. It was more serious. It was that I did not need women for what I really needed. What I had I could not share with a woman. I would want to share it but it was something which could not be shared. All I could really give were the unimportant things like a certain amount of kindness or a certain amount of sympathy or even a certain amount of real love. There was nobody anywhere I could miss enough for it to matter and the terrible thing for me was that even when I missed them I knew it was not important and that nothing had been really lost for me. That was why she had wanted it to be over. That was why she had gone back to him. She had watched me for such a long time: I loved dogs, children, toys, things like that: and she had been so surprised. She had supposed I wouldn't. Then she had realized I could leave a child as easily as a pet dog. That my attachment to things was so different from hers.

I went to the window. It was dark below, those nine stories between myself and the street. From this height the city did not look habitable; and yet it was inhabited, and I had grown up in it, and it was my native city, as much as any city anywhere was native to me. It appeared to me not so much a city as a gigantic apparatus, a machine that required an island to house it. It rusted under the dark sky.

I suppose I had known I would not send the letter, nor would I finally insist upon the alternative. It was only another of the violent things I pretended I was going to do and then did not do. It was only another of the gestures I seemed about to make and then did not make. Finally I would always stand like this, at a window, staring down nine stories toward nothingness, with some gesture broken off in my hands. She was free to go. I would not any more interfere with the life she so passionately wanted. It was useless for me to try to hold her. I was not made to hold anyone. They escaped me or I lost them. I could not maintain a sense of injustice long, or even much of a sense of betrayal. She was right. Things were for me less real than they were for her. I existed among phantoms whose natures I chose to pretend were not phantom-like. I did not really believe in those injuries I seemed to have endured. Something in me dissipated them. The justice was really all on her side. I could no more be a villain than I could be the opposite of a villain. I was not all of anything. Somewhere all my desires came apart and all my justifications turned untrue.

She understood she was free to go. The little drama, she with her threatened virtue and I with my blackmail, was over. We had lapsed back into what we always were. Nevertheless, she hesitated. She seemed preoccupied with her glove, snapping and unsnapping the clasp. She began again to speak.

She was sorry it had all ended like this. She had wanted it so to end differently. She had caused me a great deal of suffering and she had loved me and she could not understand why when there was love there was always suffering. Possibly she still loved me. It was simply that she had to do what she had to do.

We could be friends. There was no reason not to be friends. She would never have with him what it was she had had with me. There were so many things he was not. She wished desperately she could explain.

I stood there, not really listening to her, hoping now she would go. A terrible emptiness inhabited me. I was thinking that I had made what was for me a great effort toward love and I had failed and that I would not be able to make the effort again. That I had exhausted whatever strength to love I possessed. That there would be nothing for some time but this emptiness. That I would have to learn to live with it.

I became slowly aware of what it was she was saying. It took a while. She was already thinking of herself as married. She had accomplished it. The house was purchased and the sprinklers worked on the lawn. Barbara was at school. There were the long afternoons. She would miss me terribly. There was no reason for us not to see each other. I would have then no responsibility for her or for her life. I would neither have to house her nor feed her nor clothe her nor be concerned about Barbara. She would have achieved then the permanence of the order she had always wanted. It would not be as though she were being unfaithful. She would be faithful: with of course the sole exception of myself and she did not, by some logic I could not entirely follow, think of me as somebody she would be being unfaithful with. Rather I would be part of the odd scheme of how to be faithful.

So there would be the three of us, locked charmingly together, each in his necessary place. He would play the role of the solid husband, with whom she felt safe: she would be the wife, ornamental, lovely, who served the coffee to his friends: and I would occupy the special niche she was suggesting. It seemed to her so satisfactory a way out. I should really have no objections. It was so difficult for a woman to find everything she wanted neatly packaged into one man. I was quite sure that she even thought of it as one of her rights. She looked at me with a queer mixture of supplication and bravado. She was not sure how I would answer. It was something a nice girl was not supposed to suggest and she had been for so long a time a nice girl. It was how mother had reared her and how the little town she came from was organized and what one was at school and in chapel and riding in the subway and smiling across a dinner table. She was very hesitant about ending the little fiction now. She did not really feel that she was ending it. Rather she was extending the definition a bit. It was only that she wanted everything: the proper marriage and the improper love; the orderly living room and the disorderly bedroom; the sprinkler on the lawn and an appointment somewhere between two and four. I smiled. She had not expected me to smile. I smiled at her with an affection I had not experienced for her for some time. It reassured her. At least I was not being indignant or scornful or outraged. I looked at her curiously. I could see now that I had never understood her at all. She was not anything like the girl whose explanation I had sought lying on the sofa during all those terrible days I had missed her so. She was somebody whose existence I had never suspected. I wondered now if our positions had been reversed and Howard were here in the room with her as I was would she have made a proposal of such a convenient nature to him? She, of course, would not. It was even a little funny to think of her making it to him. What made her think then that she could suggest so unique an arrangement with me and there exist in her the hope, for the hope obviously existed in her, that I would accept it? She looked at me then from under her lowered eyelashes. There was the hint of a peculiar sort of smile on the little mouth, that mouth which pouted somewhat, and was so childish, so easily wounded, so apparently vulnerable to all the world.

You're different, she said. You accept things.

I looked at her fondly. She thought I was so right for the role she wanted me to play. I accepted things. I was after all an artist, that odd creature among men. I was not predictable like Howard was. I would not really harm her as he would should he ever suspect her or doubt her. I had a fatal but very accommodating tendency to forgive. I hardly ever meant anything too seriously. I did not condemn her for some unnatural desire she might show nor look at her horror-stricken when she admitted to some unorthodox sexual yearning. I was soft. My pride was of a thinner nature than his. I was perfect for that sort of afternoon when one was bored and had done all the possible shopping that could be done. I was a nice repository for her sense of sin. I was queer in the way men are who wore beards and joined walking clubs. I made her feel real the way a short stay in a brothel would: she would have always remembered how informal the life was. She would quickly establish me as an exciting stopover on her way home. I was what she could use to reconcile herself to what she thought of intermittently as dull. It was how she saw me. Really it was how she had always seen me. It was possibly how I had allowed myself to be always seen.

It was quite an overwhelming piece of character reading.

I crossed to her and lifted her from the sofa and drew her one glove back on her hand.

He's waiting for you, I said. He'll be worried about your cousin from Los Angeles. You better go.

What will you do? she said.

I'll go out.

With whom?

(She was really incorrigible!)

My grandmother, I said. From Duluth. Beat it. Go get married.

What are you smiling at? she said.

Nothing, I said.

You're smiling at something, she said. What did I say that was so funny?

I looked at her.

You'll never know, I said.

I took her arm. At the door I kissed her good-by. I patted affectionately the small firm rump I would never pat again and then she was gone, the door closed, the apartment quiet, the coffee all burned away on the small electric range, my books, my papers, my radio, all the appurtenances of my life in place, even my razor when I went into the bathroom and began to shave.

II

Here I am, the man in the hotel bar said to the pretty girl, almost forty, with a small reputation, some money in the bank, a convenient address, a telephone number easily available, this look on my face you think peculiar to me, my hand here on this table real enough, all of me real enough if one doesn't look too closely.

She's gone now, and when later people asked me how she was and what she was doing, people who knew us, I always said cheerfully that she was happily bedded down with a textile company and several chemical subsidiaries, which of course wasn't the gentlemanly thing to say. I think about her now and then, at odd moments, passing that crosstown street of hers, wondering how much chintz her bedroom has, and whether when it rains, or the earth steams around that Connecticut home she's disappeared into, she thinks of me at all. But why should she? I was only a mistake she almost made.

But then again, the man said to the pretty girl who glanced now at her wrist watch, I might be all wrong, and the world is full of raging passions I know nothing of, and Tristram is even now taking the Bronx Express home to his Isolde, and hearts, slightly nobler than mine and hers, exist in profusion. I rather think though it's the acrobat, as in my dream, with the dangerous, vanity-ridden, and meaningless life, who's most like us. At least, so it seems to me: that paltry costume, that pride because the trick's accomplished and once again he hasn't fallen. The whole point is that nothing can save us but a good fall. It's staying up there on the wire, balancing ourselves with that trivial parasol and being so pleased with terrifying an audience, that's finishing us. Don't you agree? A great fall, that's what we need.

I wish, though, the man said to the pretty girl who, having glanced at her wrist watch, finished the last of her drink and looked expectantly at him, the story had been different. Touching perhaps, or tender. It's odd though how few things are. One would have imagined there would be more. But the tenderness seems always to be incidental. It never is the main thing.

You'd like to go now, wouldn't you? the man said to the pretty girl. It's been such a long afternoon. It's nice to have someplace to go, like home, and something to do, like eat dinner, and someone to see, like a woman, and something assured, like a bed to lie down on. It's what we use as hope.

He stood up.

There's a poem I always thought I'd someday use, the man said. Do you know it? He began to quote:

Love bade me welcome, but my soul drew back, guilty of dust and sin . . .

The pretty girl did not know the poem.

They went out together.

GIOVANNI'S ROOM

James Baldwin

David, a young American in 1950s Paris, is waiting for his fiancée to return from vacation in Spain. But when he meets Giovanni, a handsome Italian barman, the two men are drawn into an intense affair. After three months David's fiancée returns, and, denying his true nature, David rejects Giovanni for a 'safe' future as a married man. His decision eventually brings tragedy.

Full of passion, regret and longing, this story of a fated love triangle has become a landmark in gay writing, but its appeal is broader. James Baldwin caused outrage as a black author writing about white homosexuals, yet for him the issues of race, sexuality and personal freedom were eternally intertwined.

'Audacious . . . remarkable . . . elegant and courageous' Caryl Phillips

THE HEART IS A LONELY HUNTER

Carson McCullers

Carson McCullers' prodigious first novel was published to instant acclaim when she was just twenty-three. Set in a small town in the middle of the deep South, it is the story of John Singer, a lonely deaf-mute, and a disparate group of people who are drawn towards his kind, sympathetic nature. The owner of the café where Singer eats every day, a young girl desperate to grow up, an angry drunkard, a frustrated black doctor: each pours their heart out to Singer, their silent confidant, and he in turn changes their disenchanted lives in ways they could never imagine.

'I cannot think of any novel that I take more pleasure in re-reading'
Jonathan Bate

MRS BRIDGE

Evan S. Connell

Mrs Bridge is a housewife and mother in Kansas City, bringing up her three children and making a home for her husband, Walter. She shops, plays bridge and goes to the country club, but as time passes she finds that her life is unfulfilling and she cannot even ask herself the questions that trouble her. And while the children grow up and become strangers to her, Mrs Bridge – kind yet bigoted, rich yet simple – is left uncertain of her place in the world.

In a series of comical, subtle and shattering vignettes, Evan S. Connell captures perfectly the contradictions, narrow margins and fear that can shadow a life of comfort.

'Very, very funny, often moving and sad, and written with an uncompromising realism that one rarely comes across' *Daily Telegraph*